DEEP WORK

Cal Newport

T0204247

piatkus

PIATKUS

First published in the US in 2016 by Grand Central Publishing,
a division of Hachette Book Group, Inc
First published in Great Britain in 2016 by Piatkus

Copyright © Cal Newport 2016

24

The moral right of the author has been asserted.

A CIP catalogue record for this book
is available from the British Library.

ISBN 978-0-349-41368-6

Printed and bound in India by
Manipal Technologies Limited, Manipal

Papers used by Piatkus are from well-managed forests
and other responsible sources.

Piatkus
An imprint of
Little, Brown Book Group
Carmelite House
50 Victoria Embankment
London EC4Y 0DZ

An Hachette UK Company
www.hachette.co.uk

www.improvementzone.co.uk

Contents

DEEP
WORK

DEEP
WORK

Introduction

In the Swiss canton of St. Gallen, near the northern banks of Lake Zurich, is a village named Bollingen. In 1922, the psychiatrist Carl Jung chose this spot to begin building a retreat. He began with a basic two-story stone house he called the Tower. After returning from a trip to India, where he observed the practice of adding meditation rooms to homes, he expanded the complex to include a private office. "In my retiring room I am by myself," Jung said of the space. "I keep the key with me all the time; no one else is allowed in there except with my permission."

In his book *Daily Rituals*, journalist Mason Currey sorted through various sources on Jung to re-create the psychiatrist's work habits at the Tower. Jung would rise at seven a.m., Currey reports, and after a big breakfast he would spend two hours of undistracted writing time in his private office. His afternoons would often consist of meditation or long walks in the surrounding countryside. There was no electricity at the Tower, so as day gave way to night, light came from oil lamps and heat from the fireplace. Jung would retire to bed by ten p.m. "The feeling of repose and renewal that I had in this tower was intense from the start," he said.

Though it's tempting to think of Bollingen Tower as a vacation home, if we put it into the context of Jung's career at this point it's clear that the lakeside retreat was not built as an escape from work. In 1922, when Jung bought the property, he could not afford to take a vacation. Only one year earlier, in 1921, he had published *Psychological Types*, a seminal book that solidified many differences that had been long developing between Jung's thinking and the ideas of his onetime friend and mentor, Sigmund Freud. To disagree with Freud in the 1920s was a bold move. To back up his book, Jung needed to stay sharp and produce a stream of smart articles and books further supporting and establishing *analytical psychology*, the eventual name for his new school of thought.

Jung's lectures and counseling practice kept him busy in Zurich—this is clear. But he wasn't satisfied with busy-ness alone. He wanted to change the way we understood the unconscious, and this goal required deeper, more careful thought than he could manage amid his hectic city lifestyle. Jung retreated to Bollingen, not to escape his professional life, but instead to advance it.

Carl Jung went on to become one of the most influential thinkers of the twentieth century. There are, of course, many reasons for his eventual success. In this book, however, I'm interested in his commitment to the following skill, which almost certainly played a key role in his accomplishments:

Deep Work: Professional activities performed in a state of distraction-free concentration that push your cognitive capabilities to their limit. These efforts create new value, improve your skill, and are hard to replicate.

Deep work is necessary to wring every last drop of value out of your current intellectual capacity. We now know from decades of research in both psychology and neuroscience that the state of mental strain that accompanies deep work is also necessary to improve your abilities. Deep work, in other words, was exactly the type of effort needed to stand out in a cognitively demanding field like academic psychiatry in the early twentieth century.

The term "deep work" is my own and is not something Carl Jung would have used, but his actions during this period were those of someone who understood the underlying concept. Jung built a tower out of stone in the woods to promote deep work in his professional life—a task that required time, energy, and money. It also took him away from more immediate pursuits. As Mason Currey writes, Jung's regular journeys to Bollingen reduced the time he spent on his clinical work, noting, "Although he had many patients who relied on him, Jung was not shy about taking time off." Deep work, though a burden to prioritize, was crucial for his goal of changing the world.

Indeed, if you study the lives of other influential figures from both distant and recent history, you'll find that a commitment to deep work is a common theme. The sixteenth-century essayist Michel de Montaigne, for example, prefigured

Jung by working in a private library he built in the southern tower guarding the stone walls of his French château, while Mark Twain wrote much of *The Adventures of Tom Sawyer* in a shed on the property of the Quarry Farm in New York, where he was spending the summer. Twain's study was so isolated from the main house that his family took to blowing a horn to attract his attention for meals.

Moving forward in history, consider the screenwriter and director Woody Allen. In the forty-four-year period between 1969 and 2013, Woody Allen wrote and directed forty-four films that received twenty-three Academy Award nominations—an absurd rate of artistic productivity. Throughout this period, Allen never owned a computer, instead completing all his writing, free from electronic distraction, on a German Olympia SM3 manual typewriter. Allen is joined in his rejection of computers by Peter Higgs, a theoretical physicist who performs his work in such disconnected isolation that journalists couldn't find him after it was announced he had won the Nobel Prize. J.K. Rowling, on the other hand, *does* use a computer, but was famously absent from social media during the writing of her Harry Potter novels—even though this period coincided with the rise of the technology and its popularity among media figures. Rowling's staff finally started a Twitter account in her name in the fall of 2009, as she was working on *The Casual Vacancy*, and for the first year and a half her only tweet read: "This is the real me, but you won't be hearing from me often I am afraid, as pen and paper is my priority at the moment."

Deep work, of course, is not limited to the historical

or technophobic. Microsoft CEO Bill Gates famously conducted "Think Weeks" twice a year, during which he would isolate himself (often in a lakeside cottage) to do nothing but read and think big thoughts. It was during a 1995 Think Week that Gates wrote his famous "Internet Tidal Wave" memo that turned Microsoft's attention to an upstart company called Netscape Communications. And in an ironic twist, Neal Stephenson, the acclaimed cyberpunk author who helped form our popular conception of the Internet age, is near impossible to reach electronically—his website offers no e-mail address and features an essay about why he is purposefully bad at using social media. Here's how he once explained the omission: "If I organize my life in such a way that I get lots of long, consecutive, uninterrupted time-chunks, I can write novels. [If I instead get interrupted a lot] what replaces it? Instead of a novel that will be around for a long time...there is a bunch of e-mail messages that I have sent out to individual persons."

The ubiquity of deep work among influential individuals is important to emphasize because it stands in sharp contrast to the behavior of most modern knowledge workers—a group that's rapidly forgetting the value of going deep.

The reason knowledge workers are losing their familiarity with deep work is well established: network tools. This is a broad category that captures communication services like e-mail and SMS, social media networks like Twitter and Facebook, and the shiny tangle of infotainment sites like BuzzFeed and Reddit. In aggregate, the rise of these tools, combined with ubiquitous access to them through smart-phones and networked office computers, has fragmented most knowledge workers' attention into slivers. A 2012 McKinsey study found that the average knowledge worker now spends more than 60 percent of the workweek engaged in electronic communication and Internet searching, with close to 30 percent of a worker's time dedicated to reading and answering e-mail alone.

This state of fragmented attention cannot accommodate deep work, which requires long periods of uninterrupted thinking. At the same time, however, modern knowledge workers are not loafing. In fact, they report that they are as busy as ever. What explains the discrepancy? A lot can be explained by another type of effort, which provides a coun-terpart to the idea of deep work:

Shallow Work: Noncognitively demanding, logistical-style tasks, often performed while distracted. These efforts tend to not create much new value in the world and are easy to replicate.

In an age of network tools, in other words, knowledge workers increasingly replace deep work with the shallow alternative—constantly sending and receiving e-mail mes-sages like human network routers, with frequent breaks for quick hits of distraction. Larger efforts that would be well served by deep thinking, such as forming a new business strategy or writing an important grant application, get frag-mented into distracted dashes that produce muted quality.

To make matters worse for depth, there's increasing evidence that this shift toward the shallow is not a choice that can be easily reversed. Spend enough time in a state of frenetic shallowness and you *permanently* reduce your capacity to perform deep work. "What the Net seems to be doing is chipping away my capacity for concentration and contemplation," admitted journalist Nicholas Carr, in an oft-cited 2008 *Atlantic* article. "[And] I'm not the only one." Carr expanded this argument into a book, *The Shallows*, which became a finalist for the Pulitzer Prize. To write *The Shallows*, appropriately enough, Carr had to move to a cabin and forcibly disconnect.

The idea that network tools are pushing our work from the deep toward the shallow is not new. *The Shallows* was just the first in a series of recent books to examine the Internet's effect on our brains and work habits. These subsequent titles include William Powers's *Hamlet's BlackBerry*, John Freeman's *The Tyranny of E-mail*, and Alex Soojung-Kin Pang's *The Distraction Addiction*—all of which agree, more or less, that network tools are distracting us from work that requires unbroken concentration, while simultaneously degrading our capacity to remain focused.

Given this existing body of evidence, I will not spend more time in this book trying to establish this point. We can, I hope, stipulate that network tools negatively impact deep work. I'll also sidestep any grand arguments about the long-term societal consequence of this shift, as such arguments tend to open impassible rifts. On one side of the debate are techno-skeptics like Jaron Lanier and John

Freeman, who suspect that many of these tools, at least in their current state, damage society, while on the other side techno-optimists like Clive Thompson argue that they're changing society, for sure, but in ways that'll make us better off. Google, for example, might reduce our memory, but we no longer *need* good memories, as in the moment we can now search for anything we need to know.

I have no stance in this philosophical debate. My interest in this matter instead veers toward a thesis of much more pragmatic and individualized interest: Our work culture's shift toward the shallow (whether you think it's philosophically good or bad) is exposing a massive economic and personal opportunity for the few who recognize the potential of resisting this trend and prioritizing depth—an opportunity that, not too long ago, was leveraged by a bored young consultant from Virginia named Jason Benn.

There are many ways to discover that you're not valuable in our economy. For Jason Benn the lesson was made clear when he realized, not long after taking a job as a financial consultant, that the vast majority of his work responsibilities could be automated by a "kludged together" Excel script.

The firm that hired Benn produced reports for banks involved in complex deals. ("It was about as interesting as it sounds," Benn joked in one of our interviews.) The report creation process required hours of manual manipulation of data in a series of Excel spreadsheets. When he first arrived, it took Benn up to six hours per report to finish this stage (the most efficient veterans at the firm could complete this task in around half the time). This didn't sit well with Benn.

"The way it was taught to me, the process seemed clunky and manually intensive," Benn recalls. He knew that Excel has a feature called macros that allows users to automate common tasks. Benn read articles on the topic and soon put together a new worksheet, wired up with a series of these macros that could take the six-hour process of manual data manipulation and replace it, essentially, with a button click. A report-writing process that originally took him a full workday could now be reduced to less than an hour.

Benn is a smart guy. He graduated from an elite college (the University of Virginia) with a degree in economics, and like many in his situation he had ambitions for his career. It didn't take him long to realize that these ambitions would be thwarted so long as his main professional skills could be captured in an Excel macro. He decided, therefore, he needed to increase his value to the world. After a period of research, Benn reached a conclusion: He would, he declared to his family, quit his job as a human spreadsheet and become a computer programmer. As is often the case with such grand plans, however, there was a hitch: Jason Benn had no idea how to write code.

As a computer scientist I can confirm an obvious point: Programming computers is hard. Most new developers dedicate a four-year college education to learning the ropes before their first job—and even then, competition for the best spots is fierce. Jason Benn didn't have this time. After his Excel epiphany, he quit his job at the financial firm and moved home to prepare for his next step. His parents were happy he had a plan, but they weren't happy about the idea that this return home might be long-term. Benn needed to learn a hard skill, and needed to do so *fast*.

It's here that Benn ran into the same problem that holds back many knowledge workers from navigating into more explosive career trajectories. Learning something complex like computer programming requires intense uninterrupted concentration on cognitively demanding concepts—the type of concentration that drove Carl Jung to the woods surrounding Lake Zurich. This task, in other words, is an act of deep work. Most knowledge workers, however, as I argued earlier in this introduction, have lost their ability to perform deep work. Benn was no exception to this trend.

"I was always getting on the Internet and checking my e-mail; I couldn't stop myself; it was a compulsion," Benn said, describing himself during the period leading up to his quitting his finance job. To emphasize his difficulty with depth, Benn told me about a project that a supervisor at the finance firm once brought to him. "They wanted me to write a business plan," he explained. Benn didn't know how to write a business plan, so he decided he would find and read five different existing plans—comparing and contrasting them to understand what was needed. This was a good idea, but Benn had a problem: "I couldn't stay focused." There were days during this period, he now admits, when he spent almost every minute ("98 percent of my time") surfing the Web. The business plan project—a chance to distinguish himself early in his career—fell to the wayside.

By the time he quit, Benn was well aware of his difficulties with deep work, so when he dedicated himself to learning how to code, he knew he had to simultaneously teach his mind how to go deep. His method was drastic but effective. "I locked myself in a room with no computer: just textbooks, notecards, and a highlighter." He would highlight the computer programming textbooks, transfer the ideas to notecards, and then practice them out loud. These periods free from electronic distraction were hard at first, but Benn gave himself no other option: He *had* to learn this material, and he made sure there was nothing in that room to distract him. Over time, however, he got better at concentrating, eventually getting to a point where he was regularly clocking five or more disconnected hours per day in the room, focused without distraction on learning this hard new skill. "I probably read something like eighteen books on the topic by the time I was done," he recalls.

After two months locked away studying, Benn attended the notoriously difficult Dev Bootcamp: a hundred-hour-a-week crash course in Web application programming. (While researching the program, Benn found a student with a PhD from Princeton who had described Dev as "the hardest thing I've ever done in my life.") Given both his preparation and his newly honed ability for deep work, Benn excelled. "Some people show up not prepared," he said. "They can't focus.

They can't learn quickly." Only half the students who started the program with Benn ended up graduating on time. Benn not only graduated, but was also the top student in his class.

The deep work paid off. Benn quickly landed a job as a developer at a San Francisco tech start-up with $25 million in venture funding and its pick of employees. When Benn quit his job as a financial consultant, only half a year earlier, he was making $40,000 a year. His new job as a computer developer paid $100,000—an amount that can continue to grow, essentially without limit in the Silicon Valley market, along with his skill level.

When I last spoke with Benn, he was thriving in his new position. A newfound devotee of deep work, he rented an apartment across the street from his office, allowing him to show up early in the morning before anyone else arrived and work without distraction. "On good days, I can get in four hours of focus before the first meeting," he told me. "Then maybe another three to four hours in the afternoon. And I do mean 'focus': no e-mail, no Hacker News [a website popular among tech types], just programming." For someone who admitted to sometimes spending up to 98 percent of his day in his old job surfing the Web, Jason Benn's transformation is nothing short of astonishing.

Jason Benn's story highlights a crucial lesson: Deep work is not some nostalgic affectation of writers and early-twentieth-century philosophers. It's instead a skill that has great value today.

There are two reasons for this value. The first has to

do with learning. We have an information economy that's dependent on complex systems that change rapidly. Some of the computer languages Benn learned, for example, didn't exist ten years ago and will likely be outdated ten years from now. Similarly, someone coming up in the field of marketing in the 1990s probably had no idea that today they'd need to master digital analytics. To remain valuable in our economy, therefore, you must master the art of quickly learning complicated things. This task requires deep work. If you don't cultivate this ability, you're likely to fall behind as technology advances.

The second reason that deep work is valuable is because the impacts of the digital network revolution cut both ways. If you can create something useful, its reachable audience (e.g., employers or customers) is essentially limitless—which greatly magnifies your reward. On the other hand, if what you're producing is mediocre, then you're in trouble, as it's too easy for your audience to find a better alternative online. Whether you're a computer programmer, writer, marketer, consultant, or entrepreneur, your situation has become similar to Jung trying to outwit Freud, or Jason Benn trying to hold his own in a hot start-up: To succeed you have to produce the absolute best stuff you're capable of producing—a task that requires depth.

The growing necessity of deep work is new. In an industrial economy, there was a small skilled labor and professional class for which deep work was crucial, but most workers could do just fine without ever cultivating an ability to concentrate without distraction. They were paid to crank widgets—and not much about their job would change in the decades they kept it. But as we shift to an information economy, more and more of our population are knowledge workers, and deep work is becoming a key currency—even if most haven't yet recognized this reality.

Deep work is not, in other words, an old-fashioned skill falling into irrelevance. It's instead a crucial ability for anyone looking to move ahead in a globally competitive information economy that tends to chew up and spit out those who aren't earning their keep. The real rewards are reserved not for those who are comfortable using Facebook (a shallow task, easily replicated), but instead for those who are comfortable building the innovative distributed systems that run the service (a decidedly deep task, hard to replicate). Deep work is so important that we might consider it, to use the phrasing of business writer Eric Barker, "the superpower of the 21st century."

We have now seen two strands of thought—one about the increasing scarcity of deep work and the other about its increasing value—which we can combine into the idea that provides the foundation for everything that follows in this book:

The Deep Work Hypothesis: The ability to perform deep work is becoming increasingly *rare* at exactly the same time it is becoming increasingly *valuable* in our economy. As a consequence, the few who cultivate this skill, and then make it the core of their working life, will thrive.

This book has two goals, pursued in two parts. The first, tackled in Part 1, is to convince you that the deep work hypothesis is true. The second, tackled in Part 2, is to teach you how to take advantage of this reality by training your brain and transforming your work habits to place deep work at the core of your professional life. Before diving into these details, however, I'll take a moment to explain how I became such a devotee of depth.

I've spent the past decade cultivating my own ability to concentrate on hard things. To understand the origins of this interest, it helps to know that I'm a theoretical computer scientist who performed my doctoral training in MIT's famed Theory of Computation group—a professional setting where the ability to focus is considered a crucial occupational skill.

During these years, I shared a graduate student office down the hall from a MacArthur "genius grant" winner—a professor who was hired at MIT before he was old enough to legally drink. It wasn't uncommon to find this theoretician sitting in the common space, staring at markings on a whiteboard, with a group of visiting scholars arrayed around him, also sitting quietly and staring. This could go on for hours. I'd go to lunch; I'd come back—still staring. This particular professor is hard to reach. He's not on Twitter and if he doesn't know you, he's unlikely to respond to your e-mail. Last year he published sixteen papers.

This type of fierce concentration permeated the atmosphere during my student years. Not surprisingly, I soon developed a similar commitment to depth. To the chagrin of both my friends and the various publicists I've worked with on my books, I've never had a Facebook or Twitter account, or any other social media presence outside of a blog. I don't Web surf and get most of my news from my home-delivered *Washington Post* and NPR. I'm also generally hard to reach: My author website doesn't provide a personal e-mail address, and I didn't own my first smartphone until 2012 (when my pregnant wife gave me an ultimatum—"you have to have a phone *that works* before our son is born").

On the other hand, my commitment to depth has rewarded me. In the ten-year period following my college graduation, I published four books, earned a PhD, wrote peer-reviewed academic papers at a high rate, and was hired as a tenure-track professor at Georgetown University. I maintained this voluminous production while rarely working past five or six p.m. during the workweek.

This compressed schedule is possible because I've invested significant effort to minimize the shallow in my life while making sure I get the most out of the time this frees up. I build my days around a core of carefully chosen deep work, with the shallow activities I absolutely cannot avoid batched into smaller bursts at the peripheries of my schedule. Three to four hours a day, five days a week, of uninterrupted and carefully directed concentration, it turns out, can produce a lot of valuable output.

My commitment to depth has also returned nonprofessional benefits. For the most part, I don't touch a computer between the time when I get home from work and the next morning when the new workday begins (the main exception being blog posts, which I like to write after my kids go to bed). This ability to fully disconnect, as opposed to the more standard practice of sneaking in a few quick work e-mail checks, or giving in to frequent surveys of social media sites, allows me to be present with my wife and two sons in the evenings, and read a surprising number of books for a busy father of two. More generally, the lack of distraction in my life tones down that background hum of nervous mental energy that seems to increasingly pervade people's daily lives. I'm comfortable being bored, and this can be a surprisingly rewarding skill—especially on a lazy D.C. summer night listening to a Nationals game slowly unfold on the radio.

———

This book is best described as an attempt to formalize and explain my attraction to depth over shallowness, and to detail the types of strategies that have helped me act on this attraction. I've committed this thinking to words, in part, to help you follow my lead in rebuilding your life around deep work—but this isn't the whole story. My other interest in distilling and clarifying these thoughts is to further develop my own practice. My recognition of the deep work hypothesis has helped me thrive, but I'm convinced that I haven't yet reached my full value-producing potential. As you struggle and ultimately triumph with the ideas and rules in the chapters ahead, you can be assured that I'm following suit—ruthlessly culling the shallow and painstakingly cultivating the intensity of my depth. (You'll learn how I fare in this book's conclusion.)

When Carl Jung wanted to revolutionize the field of psychiatry, he built a retreat in the woods. Jung's Bollingen Tower became a place where he could maintain his ability to think deeply and then apply the skill to produce work of such stunning originality that it changed the world. In the pages ahead, I'll try to convince you to join me in the effort to build our own personal Bollingen Towers; to cultivate an ability to produce real value in an increasingly distracted world; and to recognize a truth embraced by the most productive and important personalities of generations past: A deep life is a good life.

PART 1

The Idea

Chapter One

Deep Work Is Valuable

As Election Day loomed in 2012, traffic at the *New York Times* website spiked, as is normal during moments of national importance. But this time, something was different. A wildly disproportionate fraction of this traffic—more than 70 percent by some reports—was visiting a single location in the sprawling domain. It wasn't a front-page breaking news story, and it wasn't commentary from one of the paper's Pulitzer Prize–winning columnists; it was instead a blog run by a baseball stats geek turned election forecaster named Nate Silver. Less than a year later, ESPN and ABC News lured Silver away from the *Times* (which tried to retain him by promising a staff of up to a dozen writers) in a major deal that would give Silver's operation a role in everything from sports to weather to network news segments to, improbably enough, Academy Awards telecasts. Though there's debate about the methodological rigor of Silver's hand-tuned models, there are few who deny that in 2012 this thirty-five-year-old data whiz was a winner in our economy.

Another winner is David Heinemeier Hansson, a computer programming star who created the Ruby on Rails

website development framework, which currently provides
the foundation for some of the Web's most popular destina-
tions, including Twitter and Hulu. Hansson is a partner in the
influential development firm Basecamp (called 37signals until
2014). Hansson doesn't talk publicly about the magnitude of
his profit share from Basecamp or his other revenue sources,
but we can assume they're lucrative given that Hansson splits
his time between Chicago, Malibu, and Marbella, Spain,
where he dabbles in high-performance race-car driving.

Our third and final example of a clear winner in our
economy is John Doerr, a general partner in the famed Silicon Valley venture capital fund Kleiner Perkins Caufield &
Byers. Doerr helped fund many of the key companies fuel-
ing the current technological revolution, including Twitter,
Google, Amazon, Netscape, and Sun Microsystems. The
return on these investments has been astronomical: Doerr's
net worth, as of this writing, is more than $3 billion.

Why have Silver, Hansson, and Doerr done so well? There
are two types of answers to this question. The first are *micro*
in scope and focus on the personality traits and tactics that
helped drive this trio's rise. The second type of answers are
more *macro* in that they focus less on the individuals and
more on the type of work they represent. Though both
approaches to this core question are important, the macro
answers will prove most relevant to our discussion, as they
better illuminate what our current economy rewards.

To explore this macro perspective we turn to a pair of MIT
economists, Erik Brynjolfsson and Andrew McAfee, who in

their influential 2011 book, *Race Against the Machine,* provide a compelling case that among various forces at play, it's the rise of digital technology in particular that's transforming our labor markets in unexpected ways. "We are in the early throes of a Great Restructuring," Brynjolfsson and McAfee explain early in their book. "Our technologies are racing ahead but many of our skills and organizations are lagging behind." For many workers, this lag predicts bad news. As intelligent machines improve, and the gap between machine and human abilities shrinks, employers are becoming increasingly likely to hire "new machines" instead of "new people." And when only a human will do, improvements in communications and collaboration technology are making remote work easier than ever before, motivating companies to outsource key roles to stars—leaving the local talent pool underemployed.

This reality is not, however, universally grim. As Brynjolfsson and McAfee emphasize, this Great Restructuring is not *driving down* all jobs but is instead *dividing* them. Though an increasing number of people will lose in this new economy as their skill becomes automatable or easily outsourced, there are others who will not only survive, but thrive—becoming more valued (and therefore more rewarded) than before. Brynjolfsson and McAfee aren't alone in proposing this bimodal trajectory for the economy. In 2013, for example, the George Mason economist Tyler Cowen published *Average Is Over,* a book that echoes this thesis of a digital division. But what makes Brynjolfsson and McAfee's analysis particularly useful is that they proceed to identify three specific groups that will fall on the lucrative side of this divide and reap a disproportionate amount of the benefits of the Intelligent Machine Age. Not surprisingly, it's to these three groups that Silver, Hansson, and Doerr happen to belong. Let's touch on each of these groups in turn to better understand why they're suddenly so valuable.

The High-Skilled Workers

Brynjolfsson and McAfee call the group personified by Nate Silver the "high-skilled" workers. Advances such as robotics and voice recognition are automating many low-skilled positions, but as these economists emphasize, "other technologies like data visualization, analytics, high speed communications, and rapid prototyping have augmented the contributions of more abstract and data-driven reasoning, increasing the values of these jobs." In other words, those with the oracular ability to work with and tease valuable results out of increasingly complex machines will thrive. Tyler Cowen summarizes this reality more bluntly: "The key question will be: are you good at working with intelligent machines or not?"

Nate Silver, of course, with his comfort in feeding data into large databases, then siphoning it out into his mysterious Monte Carlo simulations, is the epitome of the high-skilled worker. Intelligent machines are not an obstacle to Silver's success, but instead provide its precondition.

The Superstars

The ace programmer David Heinemeier Hansson provides an example of the second group that Brynjolfsson and McAfee predict will thrive in our new economy: "superstars."

High-speed data networks and collaboration tools like e-mail and virtual meeting software have destroyed regionalism in many sectors of knowledge work. It no longer makes sense, for example, to hire a full-time programmer, put aside office space, and pay benefits, when you can instead pay one of the world's best programmers, like Hansson, for just enough time to complete the project at hand. In this scenario, you'll probably get a better result for less money, while Hansson can service many more clients per year, and will therefore also end up better off.

The fact that Hansson might be working remotely from Marbella, Spain, while your office is in Des Moines, Iowa, doesn't matter to your company, as advances in communication and collaboration technology make the process near seamless. (This reality does matter, however, to the less-skilled local programmers living in Des Moines and in need of a steady paycheck.) This same trend holds for the growing number of fields where technology makes productive remote work possible—consulting, marketing, writing, design, and so on. Once the talent market is made universally accessible, those at the peak of the market thrive while the rest suffer.

In a seminal 1981 paper, the economist Sherwin Rosen worked out the mathematics behind these "winner-take-all" markets. One of his key insights was to explicitly model talent—labeled, innocuously, with the variable q in his formulas—as a factor with "imperfect substitution," which Rosen explains as follows: "Hearing a succession of mediocre singers does not add up to a single outstanding performance." In other words, talent is not a commodity you can buy in bulk and combine to reach the needed levels: There's a premium to being the best. Therefore, if you're in a marketplace where the consumer has access to all performers, and everyone's q value is clear, the consumer will choose the very best. Even if the talent advantage of the best is small compared to the next rung down on the skill ladder, the superstars still win the bulk of the market.

In the 1980s, when Rosen studied this effect, he focused on examples like movie stars and musicians, where there existed clear markets, such as music stores and movie theaters, where an audience has access to different performers and can accurately approximate their talent before making a purchasing decision. The rapid rise of communication and collaboration technologies has transformed many other formerly local markets into a similarly universal bazaar. The small company looking for a computer programmer or public relations consultant now has access to an international marketplace of talent in the same way that the advent of the record store allowed the small-town music fan to bypass local musicians to buy albums from the world's best bands. The superstar effect, in other words, has a broader application today than Rosen could have predicted thirty years ago. An increasing number of individuals in our economy are now competing with the rock stars of their sectors.

The Owners

The final group that will thrive in our new economy—the group epitomized by John Doerr—consists of those with capital to invest in the new technologies that are driving the Great Restructuring. As we've understood since Marx, access to capital provides massive advantages. It's also true, however, that some periods offer more advantages than others. As Brynjolfsson and McAfee point out, postwar Europe was an example of a bad time to be sitting on a pile of cash, as the combination of rapid inflation and aggressive taxation wiped out old fortunes with surprising speed (what we might call the "Downton Abbey Effect").

The Great Restructuring, unlike the postwar period, *is* a particularly good time to have access to capital. To understand why, first recall that bargaining theory, a key component in standard economic thinking, argues that when money is made through the combination of capital investment and labor, the rewards are returned, roughly speaking, proportional to the input. As digital technology reduces the need for labor in many industries, the proportion of the rewards returned to those who own the intelligent machines is growing. A venture capitalist in today's economy can fund a company like Instagram, which was eventually sold for a billion dollars, while employing *only thirteen people.* When else in history could such a small amount of labor be involved in such a large amount of value? With so little input from labor, the proportion of this wealth that flows back to the machine owners—in this case, the venture investors—is without precedent. It's no wonder that a venture capitalist I interviewed for my last book admitted to me with some concern, "Everyone wants my job."

Let's pull together the threads spun so far: Current economic thinking, as I've surveyed, argues that the unprecedented growth and impact of technology are creating a massive restructuring of our economy. In this new economy, three groups will have a particular advantage: those who can work well and creatively with intelligent machines, those who are the best at what they do, and those with access to capital.

To be clear, this Great Restructuring identified by economists like Brynjolfsson, McAfee, and Cowen is not the *only* economic trend of importance at the moment, and the three groups mentioned previously are not the *only* groups who will do well, but what's important for this book's argument is that these trends, even if not alone, *are* important, and these groups, even if they are not the only such groups, *will* thrive. If you can join any of these groups, therefore, you'll do well. If you cannot, you might still do well, but your position is more precarious.

The question we must now face is the obvious one: How does one join these winners? At the risk of quelling your rising enthusiasm, I should first confess that I have no secret for quickly amassing capital and becoming the next John Doerr. (If I had such secrets, it's unlikely I'd share them in a book.) The other two winning groups, however, are accessible. How to access them is the goal we tackle next.

How to Become a Winner in the New Economy

I just identified two groups that are poised to thrive and that I claim are accessible: those who can work creatively with intelligent machines and those who are stars in their field.

What's the secret to landing in these lucrative sectors of the widening digital divide? I argue that the following two core abilities are crucial.

Two Core Abilities for Thriving
in the New Economy

1. The ability to quickly master hard things.
2. The ability to produce at an elite level, in terms of both quality and speed.

Let's begin with the first ability. To start, we must remember that we've been spoiled by the intuitive and drop-dead-simple user experience of many consumer-facing technologies, like Twitter and the iPhone. These examples, however, are consumer products, not serious tools: Most of the intelligent machines driving the Great Restructuring are significantly more complex to understand and master.

Consider Nate Silver, our earlier example of someone who thrives by working well with complicated technology. If we dive deeper into his methodology, we discover that generating data-driven election forecasts is not as easy as typing "Who will win more votes?" into a search box. He instead maintains a large database of poll results (thousands of polls from more than 250 pollsters) that he feeds into Stata, a popular statistical analysis system produced by a company called StataCorp. These are not easy tools to master. Here, for example, is the type of command you need to understand to work with a modern database like Silver uses:

```
CREATE VIEW cities AS SELECT name, population, altitude
FROM capitals UNION SELECT name, population, altitude
FROM non_capitals;
```

Databases of this type are interrogated in a language called SQL. You send them commands like the one shown here to interact with their stored information. Understanding how to manipulate these databases is subtle. The example command, for example, creates a "view": a virtual database table that pulls together data from multiple existing tables, and that can then be addressed by the SQL commands like a standard table. When to create views and how to do so well is a tricky question, one of many that you must understand and master to tease reasonable results out of real-world databases.

Sticking with our Nate Silver case study, consider the other technology he relies on: Stata. This is a powerful tool, and definitely not something you can learn intuitively after some modest tinkering. Here, for example, is a description of the features added to the most recent version of this software: "Stata 13 adds many new features such as treatment effects, multilevel GLM, power and sample size, generalized SEM, forecasting, effect sizes, Project Manager, long strings and BLOBs, and much more." Silver uses this complex software—with its generalized SEM and BLOBs—to build intricate models with interlocking parts: multiple regressions, conducted on custom parameters, which are then referenced as custom weights used in probabilistic expressions, and so on.

The point of providing these details is to emphasize that intelligent machines are complicated and hard to master.* To join the group of those who can work well with these machines, therefore, requires that you hone your ability to master hard things. And because these technologies change rapidly, this process of mastering hard things never ends: You must be able to do it quickly, again and again.

This ability to learn hard things quickly, of course, isn't just necessary for working well with intelligent machines; it also plays a key role in the attempt to become a superstar in just about any field—even those that have little to do with technology. To become a world-class yoga instructor, for example, requires that you master an increasingly complex set of physical skills. To excel in a particular area of medicine, to give another example, requires that you be able to quickly master the latest research on relevant procedures. To summarize these observations more succinctly: If you can't learn, you can't thrive.

Now consider the second core ability from the list shown earlier: producing at an elite level. If you want to become a superstar, mastering the relevant skills is necessary, but not

---

* The complex reality of the technologies that real companies leverage to get ahead emphasizes the absurdity of the now common idea that exposure to simplistic, consumer-facing products—especially in schools—somehow prepares people to succeed in a high-tech economy. Giving students iPads or allowing them to film homework assignments on YouTube prepares them for a high-tech economy about as much as playing with Hot Wheels would prepare them to thrive as auto mechanics.

sufficient. You must then transform that latent potential into tangible results that people value. Many developers, for example, can program computers well, but David Hansson, our example superstar from earlier, leveraged this ability to produce Ruby on Rails, the project that made his reputation. Ruby on Rails required Hansson to push his current skills to their limit and produce unambiguously valuable and concrete results.

This ability to produce also applies to those looking to master intelligent machines. It wasn't enough for Nate Silver to learn how to manipulate large data sets and run statistical analyses; he needed to then show that he could use this skill to tease information from these machines that a large audience cared about. Silver worked with many stats geeks during his days at *Baseball Prospectus*, but it was Silver alone who put in the effort to adapt these skills to the new and more lucrative territory of election forecasting. This provides another general observation for joining the ranks of winners in our economy: If you don't produce, you won't thrive—no matter how skilled or talented you are.

Having established two abilities that are fundamental to getting ahead in our new, technology-disrupted world, we can now ask the obvious follow-up question: How does one cultivate these core abilities? It's here that we arrive at a central thesis of this book: **The two core abilities just described depend on your ability to perform deep work.** If you haven't mastered this foundational skill, you'll struggle to learn hard things or produce at an elite level.

The dependence of these abilities on deep work isn't

immediately obvious; it requires a closer look at the science of learning, concentration, and productivity. The sections ahead provide this closer look, and by doing so will help this connection between deep work and economic success shift for you from unexpected to unimpeachable.

Deep Work Helps You Quickly Learn Hard Things

"Let your mind become a lens, thanks to the converging rays of attention; let your soul be all intent on whatever it is that is established in your mind as a dominant, wholly absorbing idea."

This advice comes from Antonin-Dalmace Sertillanges, a Dominican friar and professor of moral philosophy, who during the early part of the twentieth century penned a slim but influential volume titled *The Intellectual Life*. Sertillanges wrote the book as a guide to "the development and deepening of the mind" for those called to make a living in the world of ideas. Throughout *The Intellectual Life*, Sertillanges recognizes the necessity of mastering complicated material and helps prepare the reader for this challenge. For this reason, his book proves useful in our quest to better understand how people quickly master hard (cognitive) skills.

To understand Sertillanges's advice, let's return to the quote from earlier. In these words, which are echoed in many forms in *The Intellectual Life*, Sertillanges argues that to advance your understanding of your field you must tackle the relevant topics systematically, allowing your "converging rays of attention" to uncover the truth latent in each. In other words, he teaches: *To learn requires intense concentration*. This idea turns out to be ahead of its time. In reflecting on the life of the mind in the 1920s, Sertillanges uncovered a fact about mastering cognitively demanding tasks that would take academia another seven decades to formalize.

This task of formalization began in earnest in the 1970s, when a branch of psychology, sometimes called performance psychology, began to systematically explore what separates experts (in many different fields) from everyone else. In the early 1990s, K. Anders Ericsson, a professor at Florida State University, pulled together these strands into a single coherent answer, consistent with the growing research literature, that he gave a punchy name: deliberate practice.

Ericsson opens his seminal paper on the topic with a powerful claim: "We deny that these differences [between expert performers and normal adults] are immutable... Instead, we argue that the differences between expert performers and normal adults reflect a life-long period of deliberate effort to improve performance in a specific domain."

American culture, in particular, loves the storyline of the prodigy ("Do you know how easy this is for me!?" Matt Damon's character famously cries in the movie *Good Will Hunting* as he makes quick work of proofs that stymie the world's top mathematicians). The line of research promoted by Ericsson, and now widely accepted (with caveats*), de-

---

* After Malcolm Gladwell popularized the idea of deliberate practice in his 2008 bestseller, *Outliers: The Story of Success*, it became fashionable

stabilizes these myths. To master a cognitively demanding task requires this specific form of practice—there are few exceptions made for natural talent. (On this point too, Sertillanges seems to have been ahead of his time, arguing in *The Intellectual Life*, "Men of genius themselves were great only by bringing all their power to bear on the point on which they had decided to show their full measure." Ericsson couldn't have said it better.)

This brings us to the question of what deliberate practice actually requires. Its core components are usually identified as follows: (1) your attention is focused tightly on a specific skill you're trying to improve or an idea you're trying to master; (2) you receive feedback so you can correct your approach to keep your attention exactly where it's most productive. The first component is of particular importance to our discussion, as it emphasizes that deliberate practice cannot exist alongside distraction, and that it instead requires uninterrupted concentration. As Ericsson emphasizes, "Diffused attention

---

within psychology circles (a group suspicious, generally speaking, of all things Gladwellian) to poke holes in the deliberate practice hypothesis. For the most part, however, these studies did not invalidate the necessity of deliberate practice, but instead attempted to identify other components also playing a role in expert performance. In a 2013 journal article, titled "Why Expert Performance Is Special and Cannot Be Extrapolated from Studies of Performance in the General Population: A Response to Criticisms," and published in the journal *Intelligence* 45 (2014): 81–103, Ericsson pushed back on many of these studies. In this article, Ericsson argues, among other things, that the experimental designs of these critical papers are often flawed because they assume you can extrapolate the difference between average and above average in a given field to the difference between expert and non-expert.

is almost antithetical to the *focused attention* required by deliberate practice" (emphasis mine).

As psychologists, Ericsson and the other researchers in his field are not interested in *why* deliberate practice works; they're just identifying it as an effective behavior. In the intervening decades since Ericsson's first major papers on the topic, however, neuroscientists have been exploring the physical mechanisms that drive people's improvements on hard tasks. As the journalist Daniel Coyle surveys in his 2009 book, *The Talent Code*, these scientists increasingly believe the answer includes myelin—a layer of fatty tissue that grows around neurons, acting like an insulator that allows the cells to fire faster and cleaner. To understand the role of myelin in improvement, keep in mind that skills, be they intellectual or physical, eventually reduce down to brain circuits. This new science of performance argues that you get better at a skill as you develop more myelin around the relevant neurons, allowing the corresponding circuit to fire more effortlessly and effectively. To be great at something is to be well myelinated.

This understanding is important because it provides a neurological foundation for why deliberate practice works. By focusing intensely on a specific skill, you're forcing the specific relevant circuit to fire, again and again, in isolation. This repetitive use of a specific circuit triggers cells called oligodendrocytes to begin wrapping layers of myelin around the neurons in the circuits—effectively cementing the skill. The reason, therefore, why it's important to focus intensely on the task at hand while avoiding distraction is because this is the only way to isolate the relevant neural circuit enough to trigger useful myelination. By contrast, if you're trying to learn a complex new skill (say, SQL database management) in a state of low concentration (perhaps you also have your Facebook feed open), you're firing too many circuits simultaneously and haphazardly to isolate the group of neurons you actually want to strengthen.

In the century that has passed since Antonin-Dalmace Sertillanges first wrote about using the mind like a lens to focus rays of attention, we have advanced from this elevated metaphor to a decidedly less poetic explanation expressed in terms of oligodendrocyte cells. But this sequence of thinking about thinking points to an inescapable conclusion: To learn hard things quickly, you must focus intensely without distraction. To learn, in other words, is an act of deep work. If you're comfortable going deep, you'll be comfortable mastering the increasingly complex systems and skills needed to thrive in our economy. If you instead remain one of the many for whom depth is uncomfortable and distraction ubiquitous, you shouldn't expect these systems and skills to come easily to you.

Deep Work Helps You Produce at an Elite Level

Adam Grant produces at an elite level. When I met Grant in 2013, he was the youngest professor to be awarded tenure at the Wharton School of Business at Penn. A year later, when I started writing this chapter (and was just beginning to think about my own tenure process), the claim was updated: He's now the youngest *full professor** at Wharton.

The reason Grant advanced so quickly in his corner of academia is simple: He produces. In 2012, Grant published seven articles—all of them in major journals. This is an absurdly high rate for his field (in which professors tend to work alone or in small professional collaborations and do not have large teams of students and postdocs to support their research). In 2013, this count fell to five. This is still absurdly high, but below his recent standards. He can be excused for this dip, however, because this same year he published a book titled *Give and Take*, which popularized some of his research on relationships in business. To say that this book was successful is an understatement. It ended up featured on the cover of the *New York Times Magazine* and went on to become a massive bestseller. When Grant was awarded full professorship in 2014, he had already written more than sixty peer-reviewed publications in addition to his bestselling book.

Soon after meeting Grant, my own academic career on my mind, I couldn't help but ask him about his productivity. Fortunately for me, he was happy to share his thoughts on the subject. It turns out that Grant thinks a lot about

---

* In the United States, there are three ranks of professors: assistant, associate, and full. You're typically hired as an assistant professor and promoted to associate professor when you receive tenure. Full professorship is something that usually requires many years to achieve after tenure, if you achieve it at all.

the mechanics of producing at an elite level. He sent me, for example, a collection of PowerPoint slides from a workshop he attended with several other professors in his field. The event was focused on data-driven observations about how to produce academic work at an optimum rate. These slides included detailed pie charts of time allocation per season, a flowchart capturing relationship development with co-authors, and a suggested reading list with more than twenty titles. These business professors do not live the cliché of the absentminded academic lost in books and occasionally stumbling on a big idea. They see productivity as a scientific problem to systematically solve—a goal Adam Grant seems to have achieved.

Though Grant's productivity depends on many factors, there's one idea in particular that seems central to his method: the batching of hard but important intellectual work into long, uninterrupted stretches. Grant performs this batching at multiple levels. Within the year, he stacks his teaching into the fall semester, during which he can turn all of his attention to teaching well and being available to his students. (This method seems to work, as Grant is currently the highest-rated teacher at Wharton and the winner of multiple teaching awards.) By batching his teaching in the fall, Grant can then turn his attention fully to research in the spring and summer, and tackle this work with less distraction.

Grant also batches his attention on a smaller time scale. Within a semester dedicated to research, he alternates between periods where his door is open to students and colleagues, and periods where he isolates himself to focus completely and without distraction on a single research task. (He typically divides the writing of a scholarly paper into three discrete tasks: analyzing the data, writing a full draft, and editing the draft into something publishable.) During these periods, which can last up to three or four days, he'll often put an out-of-office auto-responder on his e-mail so correspondents will know not to expect a response. "It sometimes confuses my colleagues," he told me. "They say, 'You're not out of office, I see you in your office right now!'" But to Grant, it's important to enforce strict isolation until he completes the task at hand.

My guess is that Adam Grant doesn't work substantially more hours than the average professor at an elite research institution (generally speaking, this is a group prone to workaholism), but he still manages to produce more than just about anyone else in his field. I argue that his approach to batching helps explain this paradox. In particular, by consolidating his work into intense and uninterrupted pulses, he's leveraging the following law of productivity:

$$\text{High-Quality Work Produced} = (\text{Time Spent}) \times (\text{Intensity of Focus})$$

If you believe this formula, then Grant's habits make sense: By maximizing his intensity when he works, he maximizes the results he produces per unit of time spent working.

This is not the first time I've encountered this formulaic conception of productivity. It first came to my attention when I was researching my second book, *How to Become a Straight-A Student*, many years earlier. During that research process, I interviewed around fifty ultra-high-scoring college undergraduates from some of the country's most competitive schools. Something I noticed in these interviews is that the very best students often studied less than the group of students right below them on the GPA rankings. One of the explanations for this phenomenon turned out to be the formula detailed earlier: The best students understood the role intensity plays in productivity and therefore went out of their way to maximize their concentration—radically reducing the time required to prepare for tests or write papers, without diminishing the quality of their results.

The example of Adam Grant implies that this intensity formula applies beyond just undergraduate GPA and is also relevant to other cognitively demanding tasks. But why would this be? An interesting explanation comes from Sophie Leroy, a business professor at the University of Minnesota. In a 2009 paper, titled, intriguingly, "Why Is It So Hard to Do My Work?," Leroy introduced an effect she called *attention residue*. In the introduction to this paper, she noted that other researchers have studied the effect of multitasking—trying to accomplish multiple tasks simultaneously—on performance, but that in the modern knowledge work office, once you got to a high enough level, it was more common to find people working on multiple projects sequentially: "Going from one meeting to the next, starting to work on one project and soon after having to transition to another is just part of life in organizations," Leroy explains.

The problem this research identifies with this work strategy is that when you switch from some Task A to another Task B, your attention doesn't immediately follow—a *residue* of your attention remains stuck thinking about the original task. This residue gets especially thick if your work on Task A was unbounded and of low intensity before you switched, but even if you finish Task A before moving on, your attention remains divided for a while.

Leroy studied the effect of this attention residue on performance by forcing task switches in the laboratory. In one such experiment, for example, she started her subjects working on a set of word puzzles. In one of the trials, she would interrupt them and tell them that they needed to move on to a new and challenging task, in this case, reading résumés and making hypothetical hiring decisions. In other trials, she let the subjects finish the puzzles before giving them the next task. In between puzzling and hiring, she would deploy a quick lexical decision game to quantify the amount of residue left from the first task.* The results from this and her similar experiments were clear: "People experiencing attention residue after switching tasks are likely to demonstrate

---

* Lexical decision games flash strings of letters on the screen; some form real words, and some do not. The player has to decide as quickly as possible if the word is real or not, pressing one key to indicate "real" and another to indicate "not real." These tests allow you to quantify how much certain keywords are "activated" in the player's mind, because more activation leads the player to hit the "real word" quicker when they see it flash on the screen.

poor performance on that next task," and the more intense the residue, the worse the performance.

The concept of attention residue helps explain why the intensity formula is true and therefore helps explain Grant's productivity. By working on a single hard task for a long time without switching, Grant minimizes the negative impact of attention residue from his other obligations, allowing him to maximize performance on this one task. When Grant is working for days in isolation on a paper, in other words, he's doing so at a higher level of effectiveness than the standard professor following a more distracted strategy in which the work is repeatedly interrupted by residue-slathering interruptions.

Even if you're unable to fully replicate Grant's extreme isolation (we'll tackle different strategies for scheduling depth in Part 2), the attention residue concept is still telling because it implies that the common habit of working in a state of semi-distraction is potentially devastating to your performance. It might seem harmless to take a quick glance at your inbox every ten minutes or so. Indeed, many justify this behavior as *better* than the old practice of leaving an inbox open on the screen at all times (a straw-man habit that few follow anymore). But Leroy teaches us that this is not in fact much of an improvement. That quick check introduces a new target for your attention. Even worse, by seeing messages that you cannot deal with at the moment (which is almost always the case), you'll be forced to turn back to the primary task with a secondary task left unfinished. The attention residue left by such unresolved switches dampens your performance.

When we step back from these individual observations, we see a clear argument form: To produce at your peak level you need to work for extended periods with full concentration on a single task free from distraction. Put another way, **the type of work that optimizes your performance is deep work.** If you're not comfortable going deep for extended periods of time, it'll be difficult to get your performance to the peak levels of quality and quantity increasingly necessary to thrive professionally. Unless your talent and skills absolutely dwarf those of your competition, the deep workers among them will outproduce you.

What About Jack Dorsey?

I've now made my argument for why deep work supports abilities that are becoming increasingly important in our economy. Before we accept this conclusion, however, we must face a type of question that often arises when I discuss this topic: *What about Jack Dorsey?*

Jack Dorsey helped found Twitter. After stepping down as CEO, he then launched the payment-processing company Square. To quote a Forbes profile: "He is a disrupter on a massive scale and a repeat offender." He is also someone who does not spend a lot of time in a state of deep work. Dorsey doesn't have the luxury of long periods of uninterrupted thinking because, at the time when the Forbes profile was written, he maintained management duties at both Twitter (where he remained chairman) and Square, leading to a tightly calibrated schedule that ensures that the companies have a predictable "weekly cadence" (and that also ensures that Dorsey's time and attention are severely fractured).

Dorsey reports, for example, that he ends the average day with thirty to forty sets of meeting notes that he reviews and filters at night. In the small spaces between all these meetings, he believes in serendipitous availability. "I do a lot of my work at stand-up tables, which anyone can come up to," Dorsey said. "I get to hear all these conversations around the company."

This style of work is not deep. To use a term from our previous section, Dorsey's attention residue is likely slathered on thick as he darts from one meeting to another, letting people interrupt him freely in the brief interludes in between. And yet, we cannot say that Dorsey's work is shallow, because shallow work, as defined in the introduction, is low value and easily replicable, while what Jack Dorsey does is incredibly valuable and highly rewarded in our economy (as of this writing he was among the top one thousand richest people in the world, with a net worth over $1.1 billion).

Jack Dorsey is important to our discussion because he's an exemplar of a group we cannot ignore: individuals who thrive without depth. When I titled the motivating question of this section "What About Jack Dorsey?," I was providing a specific example of a more general query: If deep work is so important, why are there distracted people who do well? To conclude this chapter, I want to address this question so it doesn't nag at your attention as we dive deeper into the topic of depth in the pages ahead.

To start, we must first note that Jack Dorsey is a high-level executive of a large company (two companies, in fact). Individuals with such positions play a major role in the category of those who thrive without depth, because the lifestyle of such executives is famously and unavoidably distracted. Here's Kerry Trainor, CEO of Vimeo, trying to answer the question of how long he can go without e-mail: "I can go a good solid Saturday without, without...well, most of the daytime without it...I mean, I'll *check it*, but I won't necessarily respond."

At the same time, of course, these executives are better compensated and more important in the American economy today than in any other time in history. Jack Dorsey's success without depth is common at this elite level of management. Once we've stipulated this reality, we must then step back to remind ourselves that it doesn't undermine the general value of depth. Why? Because the necessity of distraction in these executives' work lives is highly specific to their particular jobs. A good chief executive is essentially a hard-to-automate decision engine, not unlike IBM's *Jeopardy!*-playing Watson system. They have built up a hard-won repository of experience and have honed and proved an instinct for their market. They're then presented inputs throughout the day—in the form of e-mails, meetings, site visits, and the like—that they must process and act on. To ask a CEO to spend four hours thinking deeply about a single problem is a waste of what makes him or her valuable. It's better to hire three smart subordinates to think deeply about the problem and then bring their solutions to the executive for a final decision.

This specificity is important because it tells us that if you're a high-level executive at a major company, you probably don't need the advice in the pages that follow. On the other hand, it also tells us that you cannot extrapolate the approach of these executives to *other* jobs. The fact that Dorsey encourages interruption or Kerry Trainor checks his e-mail constantly doesn't mean that you'll share their success if you follow suit: Their behaviors are characteristic of their specific roles as corporate officers.

This rule of specificity should be applied to similar counterexamples that come to mind while reading the rest of this book. There are, we must continually remember, certain corners of our economy where depth is not valued. In addition to executives, we can also include, for example, certain types of salesmen and lobbyists, for whom constant connection is their most valued currency. There are even those who manage to grind out distracted success in fields where depth would help.

But at the same time, don't be too hasty to label your job as necessarily non-deep. Just because your current habits make deep work difficult doesn't mean that this lack of depth is fundamental to doing your job well. In the next chapter, for example, I tell the story of a group of high-powered management consultants who were convinced that constant e-mail connectivity was necessary for them to service their clients. When a Harvard professor forced them to disconnect more regularly (as part of a research study), they found, to their surprise, that this connectivity didn't matter nearly as much as they had assumed. The clients didn't really need to reach them at all times and their performance as consultants *improved* once their attention became less fractured.

Similarly, several managers I know tried to convince me that they're most valuable when they're able to respond quickly to their teams' problems, preventing project logjams. They see their role as enabling others' productivity, not necessarily protecting their own. Follow-up discussions, however, soon uncovered that this goal didn't *really* require attention-fracturing connectivity. Indeed, many software companies now deploy the Scrum project management methodology, which replaces a lot of this ad hoc messaging with regular, highly structured, and ruthlessly efficient status meetings (often held standing up to minimize the urge to bloviate). This approach frees up more managerial time for thinking deeply about the problems their teams are tackling, often improving the overall value of what they produce.

Put another way: Deep work is not the *only* skill valuable in our economy, and it's possible to do well without fostering this ability, *but* the niches where this is advisable are increasingly rare. Unless you have strong evidence that distraction is important for your specific profession, you're best served, for the reasons argued earlier in this chapter, by giving serious consideration to depth.

Chapter Two

Deep Work Is Rare

In 2012, Facebook unveiled the plans for a new headquarters designed by Frank Gehry. At the center of this new building is what CEO Mark Zuckerberg called "the largest open floor plan in the world": More than three thousand employees will work on movable furniture spread over a ten-acre expanse. Facebook, of course, is not the only Silicon Valley heavyweight to embrace the open office concept. When Jack Dorsey, whom we met at the end of the last chapter, bought the old San Francisco Chronicle building to house Square, he configured the space so that his developers work in common spaces on long shared desks. "We encourage people to stay out in the open because we believe in serendipity—and people walking by each other teaching new things," Dorsey explained.

Another big business trend in recent years is the rise of instant messaging. A *Times* article notes that this technology is no longer the "province of chatty teenagers" and is now helping companies benefit from "new productivity gains and improvements in customer response time." A senior product manager at IBM boasts: "We send 2.5 million I.M.'s within I.B.M. each day."

One of the more successful recent entrants into the business IM space is Hall, a Silicon Valley start-up that helps employees move beyond just chat and engage in "real-time collaboration." A San Francisco–based developer I know described to me what it was like to work in a company that uses Hall. The most "efficient" employees, he explained, set up their text editor to flash an alert on their screen when a new question or comment is posted to the company's Hall account. They can then, with a sequence of practiced keystrokes, jump over to Hall, type in their thoughts, and then jump back to their coding with barely a pause. My friend seemed impressed when describing their speed.

A third trend is the push for content producers of all types to maintain a social media presence. The *New York Times*, a bastion of old-world media values, now encourages its employees to tweet—a hint taken by the more than eight hundred writers, editors, and photographers for the paper who now maintain a Twitter account. This is not outlier behavior; it's instead the new normal. When the novelist Jonathan Franzen wrote a piece for the *Guardian* calling Twitter a "coercive development" in the literary world, he was widely ridiculed as out of touch. The online magazine *Slate* called Franzen's complaints a "lonely war on the Internet" and fellow novelist Jennifer Weiner wrote a response in *The New Republic* in which she argued, "Franzen's a category of one, a lonely voice issuing *ex cathedra* edicts that can only apply to himself." The sarcastic hashtag #JonathanFranzenhates soon became a fad.

I mention these three business trends because they highlight a paradox. In the last chapter, I argued that deep work is more valuable than ever before in our shifting economy. If this is true, however, you would expect to see this skill promoted not just by ambitious individuals but also by organizations hoping to get the most out of their employees. As the examples provided emphasize, this is not happening. Many other ideas are being prioritized as more important than deep work in the business world, including, as we just encountered, serendipitous collaboration, rapid communication, and an active presence on social media.

It's bad enough that so many trends are prioritized ahead of deep work, but to add insult to injury, many of these trends actively *decrease* one's ability to go deep. Open offices, for example, might create more opportunities for collaboration,* but they do so at the cost of "massive distraction," to quote the results of experiments conducted for a British TV special titled *The Secret Life of Office Buildings.* "If you are just getting into some work and a phone goes off in the background, it ruins what you are concentrating on," said the neuroscientist who ran the experiments for the show. "Even though you are not aware at the time, the brain responds to distractions."

---

* In Part 2, I go into more detail about why this claim is not necessarily true.

Similar issues apply to the rise of real-time messaging. E-mail inboxes, in theory, can distract you only when you choose to open them, whereas instant messenger systems are meant to be always active—magnifying the impact of interruption. Gloria Mark, a professor of informatics at the University of California, Irvine, is an expert on the science of attention fragmentation. In a well-cited study, Mark and her co-authors observed knowledge workers in real offices and found that an interruption, even if short, delays the total time required to complete a task by a significant fraction. "This was reported by subjects as being very detrimental," she summarized with typical academic understatement.

Forcing content producers onto social media also has negative effects on the ability to go deep. Serious journalists, for example, need to focus on doing serious journalism—diving into complicated sources, pulling out connective threads, crafting persuasive prose—so to ask them to interrupt this deep thinking throughout the day to participate in the frothy back-and-forth of online tittering seems irrelevant (and somewhat demeaning) at best, and devastatingly distracting at worst. The respected *New Yorker* staff writer George Packer captured this fear well in an essay about why he does not tweet: "Twitter is crack for media addicts. It scares me, not because I'm morally superior to it, but because I don't think I could handle it. I'm afraid I'd end up letting my son go hungry." Tellingly, when he wrote that essay, Packer was busy writing his book *The Unwinding*, which came out soon after and promptly won the National Book Award—despite (or, perhaps, aided by) his lack of social media use.

To summarize, big trends in business today actively decrease people's ability to perform deep work, even though the benefits promised by these trends (e.g., increased serendipity, faster responses to requests, and more exposure) are arguably dwarfed by the benefits that flow from a commitment to deep work (e.g., the ability to learn hard things fast and produce at an elite level). The goal of this chapter is to explain this paradox. The rareness of deep work, I'll argue, is not due to some fundamental weakness of the habit. When we look closer at why we embrace distraction in the workplace we'll find the reasons are more arbitrary than we might expect—based on flawed thinking combined with the ambiguity and confusion that often define knowledge work. My objective is to convince you that although our current embrace of distraction is a real phenomenon, it's built on an unstable foundation and can be easily dismissed once you decide to cultivate a deep work ethic.

The Metric Black Hole

In the fall of 2012, Tom Cochran, the chief technology officer of Atlantic Media, became alarmed at how much time he seemed to spend on e-mail. So like any good techie, he decided to quantify this unease. Observing his own behavior, he measured that in a single week he received 511 e-mail messages and sent 284. This averaged to around 160 e-mails per day over a five-day workweek. Calculating further, Cochran noted that even if he managed to spend only thirty seconds per message on average, this still added up to almost an hour and a half per day dedicated to moving information around like a human network router. This seemed like a lot of time spent on something that wasn't a primary piece of his job description.

As Cochran recalls in a blog post he wrote about his experiment for the *Harvard Business Review*, these simple statistics got him thinking about the rest of his company. Just how much time were employees of Atlantic Media spending moving around information instead of focusing on the specialized tasks they were hired to perform? Determined to answer this question, Cochran gathered company-wide statistics on e-mails sent per day and the average number of words per e-mail. He then combined these numbers with the employees' average typing speed, reading speed, and salary. The result: He discovered that Atlantic Media was spending well over a million dollars a year to pay people to process e-mails, with every message sent or received tapping the company for around ninety-five cents of labor costs. "A 'free and frictionless' method of communication," Cochran summarized, "had soft costs equivalent to procuring a small company Learjet."

Tom Cochran's experiment yielded an interesting result about the literal cost of a seemingly harmless behavior. But the real importance of this story is the experiment itself, and in particular, its complexity. It turns out to be really difficult to answer a simple question such as: What's the impact of our current e-mail habits on the bottom line? Cochran had to conduct a company-wide survey and gather statistics from the IT infrastructure. He also had to pull together salary data and information on typing and reading speed, and run the whole thing through a statistical model to spit out his final result. And even then, the outcome is fungible, as it's not able to separate out, for example, how much value was *produced* by this frequent, expensive e-mail use to offset some of its cost.

This example generalizes to most behaviors that potentially impede or improve deep work. Even though we abstractly accept that distraction has costs and depth has value, these impacts, as Tom Cochran discovered, are difficult to measure. This isn't a trait unique to habits related to distraction and depth: Generally speaking, as knowledge work makes more complex demands of the labor force, it becomes harder to measure the value of an individual's efforts. The French economist Thomas Piketty made this point explicit in his study of the extreme growth of executive salaries. The enabling assumption driving his argument is that "it is objectively difficult to measure individual contributions to a firm's output." In the absence of such measures, irrational outcomes, such as executive salaries way out of proportion to the executive's marginal productivity, can occur. Even though some details of Piketty's theory are controversial, the underlying assumption that it's increasingly difficult to measure individuals' contributions is generally considered, to quote one of his critics, "undoubtedly true."

We should not, therefore, expect the bottom-line impact of depth-destroying behaviors to be easily detected. As Tom Cochran discovered, such metrics fall into an opaque region resistant to easy measurement—a region I call the *metric black hole.* Of course, just because it's hard to measure metrics related to deep work doesn't automatically lead to the conclusion that businesses will dismiss it. We have many examples of behaviors for which it's hard to measure their bottom-line impact but that nevertheless flourish in our business culture; think, for example, of the three trends that opened this chapter, or the outsize executive salaries that puzzled Thomas Piketty. But without clear metrics to support it, any business behavior is vulnerable to unstable whim and shifting forces, and in this volatile scrum deep work has fared particularly poorly.

The reality of this metric black hole is the backdrop for the arguments that follow in this chapter. In these upcoming sections, I'll describe various mind-sets and biases that have pushed business away from deep work and toward more distracting alternatives. None of these behaviors would survive long if it was clear that they were hurting the bottom line, but the metric black hole prevents this clarity and allows the shift toward distraction we increasingly encounter in the professional world.

The Principle of Least Resistance

When it comes to distracting behaviors embraced in the workplace, we must give a position of dominance to the now ubiquitous *culture of connectivity*, where one is expected to read and respond to e-mails (and related communication) quickly. In researching this topic, Harvard Business School professor Leslie Perlow found that the professionals she surveyed spent around twenty to twenty-five hours a week *outside the office* monitoring e-mail—believing it important to answer any e-mail (internal or external) within an hour of its arrival.

You might argue—as many do—that this behavior is necessary in many fast-paced businesses. But here's where things get interesting: Perlow tested this claim. In more detail, she convinced executives at the Boston Consulting Group, a high-pressure management consulting firm with an ingrained culture of connectivity, to let her fiddle with the work habits of one of their teams. She wanted to test a simple question: Does it really help your work to be constantly connected? To do so, she did something extreme: She forced each member of the team to take one day out of the workweek completely off—no connectivity to anyone inside or outside the company.

"At first, the team resisted the experiment," she recalled about one of the trials. "The partner in charge, who had been very supportive of the basic idea, was suddenly nervous about having to tell her client that each member of her team would be off one day a week." The consultants were equally nervous and worried that they were "putting their careers in jeopardy." But the team didn't lose their clients and its members did not lose their jobs. Instead, the consultants found more enjoyment in their work, better communication among themselves, more learning (as we might have predicted, given the connection between depth and skill development highlighted in the last chapter), and perhaps most important, "a better product delivered to the client."

This motivates an interesting question: Why do so many follow the lead of the Boston Consulting Group and foster a culture of connectivity even though it's likely, as Perlow found in her study, that it hurts employees' well-being and productivity, and probably doesn't help the bottom line? I think the answer can be found in the following reality of workplace behavior.

The Principle of Least Resistance: In a business setting, without clear feedback on the impact of various behaviors to the bottom line, we will tend toward behaviors that are easiest in the moment.

To return to our question about why cultures of connectivity persist, the answer, according to our principle, is because *it's easier*. There are at least two big reasons why this is true. The first concerns responsiveness to your needs. If you work in an environment where you can get an answer to a question or a specific piece of information immediately when the need arises, this makes your life easier—at least, in the moment. If you couldn't count on this quick response time you'd instead have to do more advance planning for your work, be more organized, and be prepared to put things aside for a while and turn your attention elsewhere while waiting for what you requested. All of this would make the day to day of your working life harder (even if it produced more satisfaction and a better outcome in the long term). The rise of professional instant messaging, mentioned earlier in this chapter, can be seen as this mind-set pushed toward an extreme. If receiving an e-mail reply within an hour makes your day easier, then getting an answer via instant message in under a minute would improve this gain by an order of magnitude.

The second reason that a culture of connectivity makes life easier is that it creates an environment where it becomes acceptable to run your day out of your inbox—responding to the latest missive with alacrity while others pile up behind it, all the while feeling satisfyingly productive (more on this soon). If e-mail were to move to the periphery of your workday, you'd be required to deploy a more thoughtful approach to figuring out what you should be working on and for how long. This type of planning is hard. Consider, for example, David Allen's *Getting Things Done* task-management methodology, which is a well-respected system for intelligently managing competing workplace obligations. This system proposes a *fifteen-element* flowchart for making a decision on what to do next! It's significantly easier to simply chime in on the latest cc'd e-mail thread.

I'm picking on constant connectivity as a case study in this discussion, but it's just one of many examples of business behaviors that are antithetical to depth, and likely reducing the bottom-line value produced by the company, that nonetheless thrive because, in the absence of metrics, most people fall back on what's easiest.

To name another example, consider the common practice of setting up regularly occurring meetings for projects. These meetings tend to pile up and fracture schedules to the point where sustained focus during the day becomes impossible. Why do they persist? *They're easier.* For many, these standing meetings become a simple (but blunt) form of personal organization. Instead of trying to manage their time and obligations themselves, they let the impending meeting each week force them to take some action on a given project and more generally provide a highly visible simulacrum of progress.

Also consider the frustratingly common practice of forwarding an e-mail to one or more colleagues, labeled with a short open-ended interrogative, such as: "Thoughts?" These e-mails take the sender only a handful of seconds to write but can command many minutes (if not hours, in some cases) of time and attention from their recipients to work toward a coherent response. A little more care in crafting the message by the sender could reduce the overall time spent by all parties by a significant fraction. So why are these easily avoidable and time-sucking e-mails so common? From the sender's perspective, *they're easier.* It's a way to clear something out of their inbox—at least, temporarily—with a minimum amount of energy invested.

The Principle of Least Resistance, protected from scrutiny by the metric black hole, supports work cultures that save us from the short-term discomfort of concentration and planning, at the expense of long-term satisfaction and the production of real value. By doing so, this principle drives us toward shallow work in an economy that increasingly rewards depth. It's not, however, the only trend that leverages the metric black hole to reduce depth. We must also consider the always present and always vexing demand toward "productivity," the topic we'll turn our attention to next.

Busyness as a Proxy for Productivity

There are a lot of things difficult about being a professor at a research-oriented university. But one benefit that this profession enjoys is clarity. How well or how poorly you're doing as an academic researcher can be boiled down to a simple question: Are you publishing important papers? The answer to this question can even be quantified as a single number, such as the *h-index*: a formula, named for its inventor, Jorge Hirsch, that processes your publication and citation counts into a single value that approximates your impact on your field. In computer science, for example, an h-index score above 40 is difficult to achieve and once reached is considered the mark of a strong long-term career. On the other hand, if your h-index is in single digits when your case goes up for tenure review, you're probably in trouble. Google Scholar, a tool popular among academics for finding research papers, even calculates your h-index automatically so you can be reminded, multiple times per week, precisely where you stand. (In case you're wondering, as of the morning when I'm writing this chapter, I'm a 21.)

This clarity simplifies decisions about what work habits a professor adopts or abandons. Here, for example, is the late Nobel Prize–winning physicist Richard Feynman explaining in an interview one of his less orthodox productivity strategies:

> *To do real good physics work, you do need absolute solid lengths of time . . . it needs a lot of concentration . . . if you have a job administrating anything, you don't have the time. So I have invented another myth for myself: that I'm irresponsible. I'm actively irresponsible. I tell everyone I don't do anything. If anyone asks me to be on a committee for admissions, "no," I tell them: I'm irresponsible.*

Feynman was adamant in avoiding administrative duties because he knew they would only decrease his ability to do the one thing that mattered most in his professional life: "to do real good physics work." Feynman, we can assume, was probably bad at responding to e-mails and would likely switch universities if you had tried to move him into an open office or demand that he tweet. Clarity about what matters provides clarity about what does not.

I mention the example of professors because they're somewhat exceptional among knowledge workers, most of whom don't share this transparency regarding how well they're doing their job. Here's the social critic Matthew Crawford's description of this uncertainty: "Managers themselves inhabit a bewildering psychic landscape, and are made anxious by the vague imperatives they must answer to."

Though Crawford was speaking specifically to the plight of the knowledge work middle manager, the "bewildering psychic landscape" he references applies to many positions in this sector. As Crawford describes in his 2009 ode to the trades, *Shop Class as Soulcraft*, he quit his job as a Washington, D.C., think tank director to open a motorcycle repair shop exactly to escape this bewilderment. The feeling of taking a broken machine, struggling with it, then eventually enjoying a tangible indication that he had succeeded (the bike driving out of the shop under its own power) provides a concrete sense of accomplishment he struggled to replicate when his day revolved vaguely around reports and communications strategies.

A similar reality creates problems for many knowledge workers. They want to prove that they're productive members of the team and are earning their keep, but they're not entirely clear what this goal constitutes. They have no rising h-index or rack of repaired motorcycles to point to as evidence of their worth. To overcome this gap, many seem to be turning back to the last time when productivity was more universally observable: the industrial age.

To understand this claim, recall that with the rise of assembly lines came the rise of the Efficiency Movement, identified with its founder, Frederic Taylor, who would famously stand with a stopwatch monitoring the efficiency of worker movements—looking for ways to increase the speed at which they accomplished their tasks. In Taylor's era, productivity was unambiguous: widgets created per unit of time. It seems that in today's business landscape, many knowledge workers, bereft of other ideas, are turning toward this old definition of productivity in trying to solidify their value in the otherwise bewildering landscape of their professional lives. (David Allen, for example, even uses the specific phrase "cranking widgets" to describe a productive work flow.) Knowledge workers, I'm arguing, are tending toward increasingly visible busyness because they lack a better way to demonstrate their value. Let's give this tendency a name.

Busyness as Proxy for Productivity: In the absence of clear indicators of what it means to be productive and valuable in their jobs, many knowledge workers turn back toward an industrial indicator of productivity: doing lots of stuff in a visible manner.

This mind-set provides another explanation for the popularity of many depth-destroying behaviors. If you send and answer e-mails at all hours, if you schedule and attend meetings constantly, if you weigh in on instant message systems like Hall within seconds when someone poses a new question, or if you roam your open office bouncing ideas off all whom you encounter—all of these behaviors make you seem busy in a public manner. If you're using busyness as a proxy for productivity, then these behaviors can seem crucial for convincing yourself and others that you're doing your job well.

This mind-set is not necessarily irrational. For some, their jobs really do depend on such behavior. In 2013, for example, Yahoo's new CEO Marissa Mayer banned employees from working at home. She made this decision after checking the server logs for the virtual private network that

Yahoo employees use to remotely log in to company servers. Mayer was upset because the employees working from home didn't sign in enough throughout the day. She was, in some sense, punishing her employees for not spending more time checking e-mail (one of the primary reasons to log in to the servers). "If you're not visibly busy," she signaled, "I'll assume you're not productive."

Viewed objectively, however, this concept is anachronistic. Knowledge work is not an assembly line, and extracting value from information is an activity that's often at odds with busyness, not supported by it. Remember, for example, Adam Grant, the academic from our last chapter who became the youngest full professor at Wharton by repeatedly shutting himself off from the outside world to concentrate on writing. Such behavior is the opposite of being publicly busy. If Grant worked for Yahoo, Marissa Mayer might have fired him. But this deep strategy turned out to produce a massive amount of value.

We could, of course, eliminate this anachronistic commitment to busyness if we could easily demonstrate its negative impact on the bottom line, but the metric black hole enters the scene at this point and prevents such clarity. This potent mixture of job ambiguity and lack of metrics to measure the effectiveness of different strategies allows behavior that can seem ridiculous when viewed objectively to thrive in the increasingly bewildering psychic landscape of our daily work.

As we'll see next, however, even those who have a clear understanding of what it means to succeed in their knowledge work job can still be lured away from depth. All it takes is an ideology seductive enough to convince you to discard common sense.

The Cult of the Internet

Consider Alissa Rubin. She's the *New York Times'* bureau chief in Paris. Before that she was the bureau chief in Kabul, Afghanistan, where she reported from the front lines on the postwar reconstruction. Around the time I was writing this chapter, she was publishing a series of hard-hitting articles that looked at the French government's complicity in the Rwandan genocide. Rubin, in other words, is a serious journalist who is good at her craft. She also, at what I can only assume is the persistent urging of her employer, tweets.

Rubin's Twitter profile reveals a steady and somewhat desultory string of missives, one every two to four days, as if Rubin receives a regular notice from the *Times'* social media desk (a real thing) reminding her to appease her followers. With few exceptions, the tweets simply mention an article she recently read and liked.

Rubin is a reporter, not a media personality. Her value to her paper is her ability to cultivate important sources, pull together facts, and write articles that make a splash. It's the Alissa Rubins of the world who provide the *Times* with its reputation, and it's this reputation that provides the foundation for the paper's commercial success in an age of ubiquitous and addictive click-bait. So why is Alissa Rubin urged to regularly interrupt this necessarily deep work to provide, for free, shallow content to a service run by an unrelated media company based out of Silicon Valley? And perhaps even more important, why does this behavior seem so normal to most people? If we can answer these questions, we'll better understand the final trend I want to discuss relevant to the question of why deep work has become so paradoxically rare.

A foundation for our answer can be found in a warning provided by the late communication theorist and New York University professor Neil Postman. Writing in the early 1990s, as the personal computer revolution first accelerated, Postman argued that our society was sliding into a troubling relationship with technology. We were, he noted, no longer discussing the trade-offs surrounding new technologies, balancing the new efficiencies against the new problems introduced. If it's high-tech, we began to instead assume, then it's good. Case closed.

He called such a culture a *technopoly*, and he didn't mince words in warning against it. "Technopoly eliminates alternatives to itself in precisely the way Aldous Huxley outlined in *Brave New World*," he argued in his 1993 book on the topic. "It does not make them illegal. It does not make them immoral. It does not even make them unpopular. It makes them invisible and therefore irrelevant."

Postman died in 2003, but if he were alive today he would likely express amazement about how quickly his fears from the 1990s came to fruition—a slide driven by the unforeseen and sudden rise of the Internet. Fortunately, Postman has an intellectual heir to continue this argument in the

Internet Age: the hypercitational social critic Evgeny Morozov. In his 2013 book, *To Save Everything, Click Here*, Morozov attempts to pull back the curtains on our technopolic obsession with "the Internet" (a term he purposefully places in scare quotes to emphasize its role as an ideology), saying: "It's this propensity to view 'the Internet' as a source of wisdom and policy advice that transforms it from a fairly uninteresting set of cables and network routers into a seductive and exciting ideology—perhaps today's uber-ideology."

In Morozov's critique, we've made "the Internet" synonymous with the revolutionary future of business and government. To make your company more like "the Internet" is to be with the times, and to ignore these trends is to be the proverbial buggy-whip maker in an automotive age. We no longer see Internet tools as products released by for-profit companies, funded by investors hoping to make a return, and run by twentysomethings who are often making things up as they go along. We're instead quick to idolize these digital doodads as a signifier of progress and a harbinger of a (dare I say, brave) new world.

This Internet-centrism (to steal another Morozov term) is what technopoly looks like today. It's important that we recognize this reality because it explains the question that opened this section. The *New York Times* maintains a social media desk and pressures its writers, like Alissa Rubin, toward distracting behavior, because in an Internet-centric technopoly such behavior is not up for discussion. The alternative, to not embrace all things Internet, is, as Postman would say, "invisible and therefore irrelevant."

This invisibility explains the uproar, mentioned earlier, that arose when Jonathan Franzen dared suggest that novelists shouldn't tweet. It riled people not because they're well versed in book marketing and disagreed with Franzen's conclusion, but because it surprised them that anyone serious would suggest the irrelevance of social media. In an Internet-centric technopoly such a statement is the equivalent of a flag burning—desecration, not debate.

Perhaps the near universal reach of this mind-set is best captured in an experience I had recently on my commute to the Georgetown campus where I work. Waiting for the light to change so I could cross Connecticut Avenue, I idled behind a truck from a refrigerated supply chain logistics company. Refrigerated shipping is a complex, competitive business that requires equal skill managing trade unions and route scheduling. It's the ultimate old-school industry and in many ways is the opposite of the lean consumer-facing tech start-ups that currently receive so much attention. What struck me as I waited in traffic behind this truck, however, was not the complexity or scale of this company, but instead a graphic that had been commissioned and then affixed, probably at significant expense, on the back of this entire fleet of trucks—a graphic that read: "like us on Facebook."

Deep work is at a severe disadvantage in a technopoly because it builds on values like quality, craftsmanship, and mastery that are decidedly old-fashioned and nontechnological. Even worse, to support deep work often requires the rejection of much of what is new and high-tech. Deep work is exiled in favor of more distracting high-tech behaviors,

like the professional use of social media, not because the former is empirically inferior to the latter. Indeed, if we had
hard metrics relating the impact of these behaviors on the
bottom line, our current technopoly would likely crumble.
But the metric black hole prevents such clarity and allows us
instead to elevate all things Internet into Morozov's feared
"uber-ideology." In such a culture, we should not be surprised that deep work struggles to compete against the shiny
thrum of tweets, likes, tagged photos, walls, posts, and all
the other behaviors that we're now taught are necessary for
no other reason than that they exist.

Bad for Business. Good for You.

Deep work *should* be a priority in today's business climate.
But it's not. I've just summarized various explanations for
this paradox. Among them are the realities that deep work is
hard and shallow work is easier, that in the absence of clear
goals for your job, the visible busyness that surrounds shallow work becomes self-preserving, and that our culture has
developed a belief that if a behavior relates to "the Internet,"
then it's good—regardless of its impact on our ability to produce valuable things. All of these trends are enabled by the
difficulty of directly measuring the value of depth or the cost
of ignoring it.

If you believe in the value of depth, this reality spells bad
news for businesses in general, as it's leading them to miss out
on potentially massive increases in their value production.
But for *you*, as an individual, good news lurks. The myopia

of your peers and employers uncovers a great personal advantage. Assuming the trends outlined here continue, depth will become increasingly rare and therefore increasingly valuable. Having just established that there's nothing fundamentally flawed about deep work and nothing fundamentally necessary about the distracting behaviors that displace it, you can therefore continue with confidence with the ultimate goal of this book: to systematically develop your personal ability to go deep—and by doing so, reap great rewards.

Chapter Three

Deep Work Is Meaningful

Ric Furrer is a blacksmith. He specializes in ancient and medieval metalworking practices, which he painstakingly re-creates in his shop, Door County Forgeworks. "I do all my work by hand and use tools that multiply my force without limiting my creativity or interaction with the material," he explains in his artist's statement. "What may take me 100 blows by hand can be accomplished in one by a large swaging machine. This is the antithesis of my goal and to that end all my work shows evidence of the two hands that made it."

A 2012 PBS documentary provides a glimpse into Furrer's world. We learn that he works in a converted barn in Wisconsin farm country, not far inland from the scenic Sturgeon Bay of Lake Michigan. Furrer often leaves the barn doors open (to vent the heat of the forges, one suspects), his efforts framed by farm fields stretching to the horizon. The setting is idyllic but the work can seem, at first encounter, brutish. In the documentary, Furrer is trying to re-create a Viking-era sword. He begins by using a fifteen-hundred-year-old technique to smelt *crucible steel*: an unusually pure (for the period) form of the metal. The result is an ingot, not much bigger than three or four stacked smartphones. This dense ingot must then be shaped and polished into a long and elegant sword blade.

"This part, the initial breakdown, is terrible," Furrer says to the camera as he methodically heats the ingot, hits it with a hammer, turns it, hits it, then puts it back in the flames to start over. The narrator reveals that it will take *eight hours* of this hammering to complete the shaping. As you watch Furrer work, however, the sense of the labor shifts. It becomes clear that he's not drearily whacking at the metal like a miner with a pickaxe: Every hit, though forceful, is carefully controlled. He peers intently at the metal, through thin-framed intellectual glasses (which seem out of place perched above his heavy beard and broad shoulders), turning it *just so* for each impact. "You have to be very gentle with it or you will crack it," he explains. After a few more hammer strikes, he adds: "You have to nudge it; slowly it breaks down; then you start to enjoy it."

At one point about halfway through the smithing, after Furrer has finished hammering out the desired shape, he begins rotating the metal carefully in a narrow trough of burning charcoal. As he stares at the blade something clicks: "It's ready." He lifts the sword, red with heat, holding it away from his body as he strides swiftly toward a pipe filled with oil and plunges in the blade to cool it. After a moment of relief that the blade did not crack into pieces—a common occurrence at this step—Furrer pulls it from the oil. The residual heat of the metal lights the fuel, engulfing the sword's full length in yellow flames. Furrer holds the burning sword up above his head with a single powerful arm and stares at it a moment before blowing out the fire. During this brief pause, the flames illuminate his face, and his admiration is palpable.

"To do it right, it is the most complicated thing I know how to make," Furrer explains. "And it's that challenge that drives me. I don't need a sword. But I *have* to make them."

Ric Furrer is a master craftsman whose work requires him to spend most of his day in a state of depth—even a small slip in concentration can ruin dozens of hours of effort. He's also someone who clearly finds great meaning in his profession. This connection between deep work and a good life is familiar and widely accepted when considering the world of craftsmen. "The satisfactions of manifesting oneself concretely in the world through manual competence have been known to make a man quiet and easy," explains Matthew Crawford. And we believe him.

But when we shift our attention to knowledge work this connection is muddied. Part of the issue is clarity. Craftsmen like Furrer tackle professional challenges that are simple to define but difficult to execute—a useful imbalance when seeking purpose. Knowledge work exchanges this clarity for ambiguity. It can be hard to define exactly what a given knowledge worker does and how it differs from another: On our worst days, it can seem that *all* knowledge work boils down to the same exhausting roil of e-mails and PowerPoint, with only the charts used in the slides differentiating one career from another. Furrer himself identifies this blandness when he writes: "The world of information superhighways and cyber space has left me rather cold and disenchanted."

Another issue muddying the connection between depth and meaning in knowledge work is the cacophony of voices attempting to convince knowledge workers to spend more time engaged in shallow activities. As elaborated in the last chapter, we live in an era where anything Internet related is understood by default to be innovative and necessary. Depth-destroying behaviors such as immediate e-mail responses and an active social media presence are lauded, while avoidance of these trends generates suspicion. No one would fault Ric Furrer for not using Facebook, but if a knowledge worker makes this same decision, then he's labeled an eccentric (as I've learned from personal experience).

Just because this connection between depth and meaning is less clear in knowledge work, however, doesn't mean that it's nonexistent. The goal of this chapter is to convince you that deep work *can* generate as much satisfaction in an information economy as it so clearly does in a craft economy. In the sections ahead, I'll make three arguments to support this claim. These arguments roughly follow a trajectory from the conceptually narrow to broad: starting with a neurological perspective, moving to the psychological, and ending with the philosophical. I'll show that regardless of the angle from which you attack the issue of depth and knowledge work, it's clear that by embracing depth over shallowness you can tap the same veins of meaning that drive craftsmen like Ric Furrer. The thesis of this final chapter in Part 1, therefore, is that a deep life is not just economically lucrative, but also a life well lived.

A Neurological Argument for Depth

The science writer Winifred Gallagher stumbled onto a connection between attention and happiness after an unexpected and terrifying event, a cancer diagnosis—"not just cancer," she clarifies, "but a particularly nasty, fairly advanced kind." As Gallagher recalls in her 2009 book *Rapt*, as she walked away from the hospital after the diagnosis she formed a sudden and strong intuition: "This disease wanted to monopolize my attention, but as much as possible, I would focus on my life instead." The cancer treatment that followed was exhausting and terrible, but Gallagher couldn't help noticing, in that corner of her brain honed by a career in nonfiction writing, that her commitment to focus on what was good in her life—"movies, walks, and a 6:30 martini"—worked surprisingly well. Her life during this period should have been mired in fear and pity, but it was instead, she noted, often quite pleasant.

Her curiosity piqued, Gallagher set out to better understand the role that attention—that is, what we choose to focus on and what we choose to ignore—plays in defining the quality of our life. After five years of science reporting, she came away convinced that she was witness to a "grand unified theory" of the mind:

Like fingers pointing to the moon, other diverse disciplines from anthropology to education, behavioral economics to family counseling, similarly suggest that the skillful management of attention is the sine qua non of the good life and the key to improving virtually every aspect of your experience.

This concept upends the way most people think about their subjective experience of life. We tend to place a lot of emphasis on our *circumstances*, assuming that what happens to us (or fails to happen) determines how we feel. From this perspective, the small-scale details of how you spend your day aren't that important, because what matters are the large-scale outcomes, such as whether or not you get a promotion or move to that nicer apartment. According to Gallagher, decades of research contradict this understanding. Our brains instead construct our worldview based on *what we pay attention to.* If you focus on a cancer diagnosis, you and your life become unhappy and dark, but if you focus instead on an evening martini, you and your life become more pleasant—even though the circumstances in both scenarios are the same. As Gallagher summarizes: "Who you are, what you think, feel, and do, what you love—is the sum of what you focus on."

In *Rapt*, Gallagher surveys the research supporting this understanding of the mind. She cites, for example, the University of North Carolina psychologist Barbara Fredrickson: a researcher who specializes in the cognitive appraisal of emotions. After a bad or disrupting occurrence in your life,

Fredrickson's research shows, what you choose to focus on exerts significant leverage on your attitude going forward. These simple choices can provide a "reset button" to your emotions. She provides the example of a couple fighting over inequitable splitting of household chores. "Rather than continuing to focus on your partner's selfishness and sloth," she suggests, "you might focus on the fact that at least a festering conflict has been aired, which is the first step toward a solution to the problem, and to your improved mood." This seems like a simple exhortation to look on the bright side, but Fredrickson found that skillful use of these emotional "leverage points" can generate a significantly more positive outcome after negative events.

Scientists can watch this effect in action all the way down to the neurological level. Stanford psychologist Laura Carstensen, to name one such example, used an fMRI scanner to study the brain behavior of subjects presented with both positive and negative imagery. She found that for young people, their amygdala (a center of emotion) fired with activity at both types of imagery. When she instead scanned the elderly, the amygdala fired only for the positive images. Carstensen hypothesizes that the elderly subjects had trained the prefrontal cortex to inhibit the amygdala in the presence of negative stimuli. These elderly subjects were not happier because their life circumstances were better than those of the young subjects; they were instead happier because they had rewired their brains to ignore the negative and savor the positive. By skillfully managing their attention, they improved their world without changing anything concrete about it.

————————

We can now step back and use Gallagher's grand theory to better understand the role of deep work in cultivating a good life. This theory tells us that your world is the outcome of what you pay attention to, so consider for a moment the type of mental world constructed when you dedicate significant time to deep endeavors. There's a gravity and sense of importance inherent in deep work—whether you're Ric Furrer smithing a sword or a computer programmer optimizing an algorithm. Gallagher's theory, therefore, predicts that if you spend enough time in this state, your mind will understand your world as rich in meaning and importance.

There is, however, a hidden but equally important benefit to cultivating rapt attention in your workday: Such concentration hijacks your attention apparatus, preventing you from noticing the many smaller and less pleasant things that unavoidably and persistently populate our lives. (The psychologist Mihaly Csikszentmihalyi, whom we'll learn more about in the next section, explicitly identifies this advantage when he emphasizes the advantage of cultivating "concentration so intense that there is no attention left over to think about anything irrelevant, or to worry about problems.") This danger is especially pronounced in knowledge work, which due to its dependence on ubiquitous connectivity generates a devastatingly appealing buffet of distraction—most of which will, if given enough attention, leach meaning and importance from the world constructed by your mind.

To help make this claim more concrete I'll use myself as a test case. Consider, for example, the last five e-mails I sent before I began writing the first draft of this chapter. Following are the subject lines of these messages along with summaries of their contents:

- **Re: URGENT calnewport Brand Registration Confirmation.** This message was in response to a standard scam in which a company tries to trick website owners into registering their domain in China. I was annoyed that they kept spamming me, so I lost my cool and responded (futilely, of course) by telling them their scam would be more convincing if they spelled "website" correctly in their e-mails.

- **Re: S R.** This message was a conversation with a family member about an article he saw in the *Wall Street Journal*.

- **Re: Important Advice.** This e-mail was part of a conversation about optimal retirement investment strategies.

- **Re: Fwd: Study Hacks.** This e-mail was part of a conversation in which I was attempting to find a time to meet with someone I know who was visiting my city—a task complicated by his fractured schedule during his visit.

- **Re: just curious.** This message was part of a conversation in which a colleague and I were reacting to some thorny office politics issues (of the type that are frequent and clichéd in academic departments).

These e-mails provide a nice case study of the type of shallow concerns that vie for your attention in a knowledge work setting. Some of the issues presented in these sample messages are benign, such as discussing an interesting article, some are vaguely stressful, such as the conversation on retirement savings strategies (a type of conversation which almost always concludes with you *not* doing the right things), some are frustrating, such as trying to arrange a meeting around busy schedules, and some are explicitly negative, such as angry responses to scammers or worried discussions about office politics.

Many knowledge workers spend most of their working day interacting with these types of shallow concerns. Even when they're required to complete something more involved, the habit of frequently checking inboxes ensures that these issues remain at the forefront of their attention. Gallagher teaches us that this is a foolhardy way to go about your day, as it ensures that your mind will construct an understanding of your working life that's dominated by stress, irritation, frustration, and triviality. The world represented by your inbox, in other words, isn't a pleasant world to inhabit.

Even if your colleagues are all genial and your interactions are always upbeat and positive, by allowing your attention to drift over the seductive landscape of the shallow, you run the risk of falling into another neurological trap identified by Gallagher: "Five years of reporting on attention have confirmed some home truths," Gallagher reports. "[Among them is the notion that] 'the idle mind is the devil's workshop'... when you lose focus, your mind tends to fix on what could be wrong with your life instead of what's right." A workday driven by the shallow, from a neurological perspective, is likely to be a draining and upsetting day, even if most of the shallow things that capture your attention seem harmless or fun.

The implication of these findings is clear. In work (and especially knowledge work), to increase the time you spend in a state of depth is to leverage the complex machinery of the human brain in a way that for several different neurological reasons maximizes the meaning and satisfaction you'll associate with your working life. "After running my tough experiment [with cancer]... I have a plan for living the rest of my life," Gallagher concludes in her book. "I'll choose my targets with care... then give them my rapt attention. In short, I'll live the focused life, because it's the best kind there is." We'd be wise to follow her lead.

A Psychological Argument for Depth

Our second argument for why depth generates meaning comes from the work of one of the world's best-known (and most misspelled) psychologists, Mihaly Csikszentmihalyi. In the early 1980s, Csikszentmihalyi, working with Reed Larson, a young colleague at the University of Chicago, invented a new technique for understanding the psychological impact of everyday behaviors. At the time, it was difficult to accurately measure the psychological impact of different activities. If you brought someone into a laboratory and asked her to remember how she felt at a specific point many hours ago, she was unlikely to recall. If you instead gave her a diary and asked her to record how she felt throughout the day, she wouldn't be likely to keep up the entries with diligence—it's simply too much work.

Csikszentmihalyi and Larson's breakthrough was to leverage new technology (for the time) to bring the question to the subject right when it mattered. In more detail, they outfitted experimental subjects with pagers. These pagers would beep at randomly selected intervals (in modern incarnations of this method, smartphone apps play the same role). When the beeper went off, the subjects would record what they were doing at the exact moment and how they felt. In some cases, they would be provided with a journal in which to record this information while in others they would be given a phone number to call to answer questions posed by a field-worker. Because the beeps were only occasional but hard to ignore, the subjects were likely to follow through with the experimental procedure. And because the subjects were recording responses about an activity *at the very moment* they were engaged in it, the responses were more accurate. Csikszentmihalyi and Larson called the approach the experience sampling method (ESM), and it provided unprecedented insight into how we actually feel about the beats of our daily lives.

Among many breakthroughs, Csikszentmihalyi's work with ESM helped validate a theory he had been developing over the preceding decade: "The best moments usually occur when a person's body or mind is stretched to its limits in a voluntary effort to accomplish something difficult and worthwhile." Csikszentmihalyi calls this mental state *flow* (a term he popularized with a 1990 book of the same title). At the time, this finding pushed back against conventional wisdom. Most people assumed (and still do) that relaxation makes them happy. We want to work less and spend more time in the hammock. But the results from Csikszentmihalyi's ESM studies reveal that most people have this wrong:

> *Ironically, jobs are actually easier to enjoy than free time, because like flow activities they have built-in goals, feedback rules, and challenges, all of which encourage one to become involved in one's work, to concentrate and lose oneself in it. Free time, on the other hand, is unstructured, and requires much greater effort to be shaped into something that can be enjoyed.*

When measured empirically, people were happier at work and less happy relaxing than they suspected. And as the ESM studies confirmed, the more such flow experiences that occur in a given week, the higher the subject's life satisfaction. Human beings, it seems, are at their best when immersed deeply in something challenging.

There is, of course, overlap between the theory of flow and the ideas of Winifred Gallagher highlighted in the last section. Both point toward the importance of depth over shallowness, but they focus on two different explanations for this importance. Gallagher's writing emphasizes that the *content* of what we focus on matters. If we give rapt attention to important things, and therefore also ignore shallow negative things, we'll experience our working life as more important and positive. Csikszentmihalyi's theory of flow, by contrast, is mostly agnostic to the content of our attention. Though he would likely agree with the research cited by Gallagher, his theory notes that the feeling of going deep is *in itself* very rewarding. Our minds like this challenge, regardless of the subject.

The connection between deep work and flow should be clear: Deep work is an activity well suited to generate a flow state (the phrases used by Csikszentmihalyi to describe what generates flow include notions of stretching your mind to its limits, concentrating, and losing yourself in an activity—all of which also describe deep work). And as we just learned, flow generates happiness. Combining these two ideas we get a powerful argument from psychology in favor of depth. Decades of research stemming from Csikszentmihalyi's original ESM experiments validate that the act of going deep orders the consciousness in a way that makes life worthwhile. Csikszentmihalyi even goes so far as to argue that modern companies should embrace this reality, suggesting that "jobs should be redesigned so that they resemble as closely as possible flow activities." Noting, however, that such a redesign would be difficult and disruptive (see, for example, my arguments from the previous chapter), Csikszentmihalyi then explains that it's even more important that the *individual*

learn how to seek out opportunities for flow. This, ultimately, is the lesson to come away with from our brief foray
into the world of experimental psychology: To build your
working life around the experience of flow produced by deep
work is a proven path to deep satisfaction.

A Philosophical Argument for Depth

Our final argument for the connection between depth and
meaning requires us to step back from the more concrete
worlds of neuroscience and psychology and instead adopt a
philosophical perspective. I'll turn for help in this discussion
to a pair of scholars who know this topic well: Hubert Dreyfus, who taught philosophy at Berkeley for more than four
decades, and Sean Dorrance Kelly, who at the time of this
writing is the chair of Harvard's philosophy department. In
2011, Dreyfus and Kelly published a book, *All Things Shining*, which explores how notions of sacredness and meaning have evolved throughout the history of human culture.
They set out to reconstruct this history because they're worried about its endpoint in our current era. "The world used
to be, in its various forms, a world of sacred, shining things,"
Dreyfus and Kelly explain early in the book. "The shining
things now seem far away."

What happened between then and now? The short
answer, the authors argue, is Descartes. From Descartes's
skepticism came the radical belief that the individual seeking certainty trumped a God or king bestowing truth.
The resulting Enlightenment, of course, led to the concept

of human rights and freed many from oppression. But as Dreyfus and Kelly emphasize, for all its good in the political arena, in the domain of the metaphysical this thinking stripped the world of the order and sacredness essential to creating meaning. In a post-Enlightenment world we have tasked *ourselves* to identify what's meaningful and what's not, an exercise that can seem arbitrary and induce a creeping nihilism. "The Enlightenment's metaphysical embrace of the autonomous individual leads not just to a boring life," Dreyfus and Kelly worry; "it leads almost inevitably to a nearly unlivable one."

This problem might at first seem far removed from our quest to understand the satisfaction of depth, but when we proceed to Dreyfus and Kelly's solution, we will discover rich new insights into the sources of meaning in professional pursuits. This connection should seem less surprising when it's revealed that Dreyfus and Kelly's response to modern nihilism builds on the very subject that opened this chapter: the craftsman.

Craftsmanship, Dreyfus and Kelly argue in their book's conclusion, provides a key to reopening a sense of sacredness in a responsible manner. To illustrate this claim, they use as an organizing example an account of a master wheelwright—the now lost profession of shaping wooden wagon wheels. "Because each piece of wood is distinct, it has its own personality," they write after a passage describing the details of the wheelwright's craft. "The woodworker has an intimate relationship with the wood he works. Its subtle virtues call out to be cultivated and cared for." In this appreciation for the "subtle virtues" of his medium, they note, the craftsman has stumbled onto something crucial in a post-Enlightenment world: a source of meaning sited outside the individual. The wheelwright doesn't decide arbitrarily which virtues of the wood he works are valuable and which are not; this value is inherent in the wood and the task it's meant to perform.

As Dreyfus and Kelly explain, such sacredness is common to craftsmanship. The task of a craftsman, they conclude, "is not to *generate* meaning, but rather to *cultivate* in himself the skill of *discerning* the meanings that are *already there*." This frees the craftsman of the nihilism of autonomous individualism, providing an ordered world of meaning. At the same time, this meaning seems safer than the sources cited in previous eras. The wheelwright, the authors imply, cannot easily use the inherent quality of a piece of pine to justify a despotic monarchy.

Returning to the question of professional satisfaction, Dreyfus and Kelly's interpretation of craftsmanship as a path to meaning provides a nuanced understanding of why the work of those like Ric Furrer resonates with so many of us. The look of satisfaction on Furrer's face as he works to extract artistry from crude metals, these philosophers would argue, is a look expressing appreciation for something elusive and valuable in modernity: a glimpse of the sacred.

Once understood, we can connect this sacredness inherent in traditional craftsmanship to the world of knowledge work. To do so, there are two key observations we must first make. The first might be obvious but requires emphasis:

There's nothing intrinsic about the *manual* trades when it comes to generating this particular source of meaning. Any pursuit—be it physical or cognitive—that supports high levels of skill can also generate a sense of sacredness.

To elaborate this point, let's jump from the old-fashioned examples of carving wood or smithing metal to the modern example of computer programming. Consider this quote from the coding prodigy Santiago Gonzalez describing his work to an interviewer:

> *Beautiful code is short and concise, so if you were to give that code to another programmer they would say, "oh, that's well written code." It's much like as if you were writing a poem.*

Gonzalez discusses computer programming similarly to the way woodworkers discuss their craft in the passages quoted by Dreyfus and Kelly.

The Pragmatic Programmer, a well-regarded book in the computer programming field, makes this connection between code and old-style craftsmanship more directly by quoting the medieval quarry worker's creed in its preface: "We who cut mere stones must always be envisioning cathedrals." The book then elaborates that computer programmers must see their work in the same way:

> *Within the overall structure of a project there is always room for individuality and craftsmanship . . . One hundred years from now, our engineering may seem as*

archaic as the techniques used by medieval cathedral builders seem to today's civil engineers, while our craftsmanship will still be honored.

You don't, in other words, need to be toiling in an open-air barn for your efforts to be considered the type of craftsmanship that can generate Dreyfus and Kelly's meaning. A similar potential for craftsmanship can be found in most skilled jobs in the information economy. Whether you're a writer, marketer, consultant, or lawyer: Your work is craft, and if you hone your ability and apply it with respect and care, then like the skilled wheelwright you can generate meaning in the daily efforts of your professional life.

It's here that some might respond that *their* knowledge work job cannot possibly become such a source of meaning because their job's subject is much too mundane. But this is flawed thinking that our consideration of traditional craftsmanship can help correct. In our current culture, we place a lot of emphasis on job description. Our obsession with the advice to "follow your passion" (the subject of my last book), for example, is motivated by the (flawed) idea that what matters most for your career satisfaction is the specifics of the job you choose. In this way of thinking, there are some rarified jobs that can be a source of satisfaction—perhaps working in a nonprofit or starting a software company—while all others are soulless and bland. The philosophy of Dreyfus and Kelly frees us from such traps. The craftsmen they cite don't have rarified jobs. Throughout most of human history, to be a blacksmith or a wheelwright wasn't glamorous. But this doesn't matter, as the specifics of the work are irrelevant. The meaning uncovered by such efforts is due to the skill and appreciation inherent in craftsmanship—not the outcomes of their work. Put another way, a wooden wheel is not noble, but its shaping can be. The same applies to knowledge work. You don't need a rarified job; you need instead a rarified approach to your work.

The second key observation about this line of argument is that cultivating craftsmanship is necessarily a deep task and therefore requires a commitment to deep work. (Recall that I argued in Chapter 1 that deep work is necessary to hone skills and to then apply them at an elite level—the core activities in craft.) Deep work, therefore, is key to extracting meaning from your profession in the manner described by Dreyfus and Kelly. It follows that to embrace deep work in your own career, and to direct it toward cultivating your skill, is an effort that can transform a knowledge work job from a distracted, draining obligation into something satisfying—a portal to a world full of shining, wondrous things.

Homo Sapiens Deepensis

The first two chapters of Part 1 were pragmatic. They argued that deep work is becoming increasingly valuable in our economy at the same time that it also is becoming increasingly rare (for somewhat arbitrary reasons). This represents a classic market mismatch: If you cultivate this skill, you'll thrive professionally.

This final chapter, by contrast, has little to add to this practical discussion of workplace advancement, *and yet* it's absolutely necessary for these earlier ideas to gain traction. The pages ahead describe a rigorous program for transforming your professional life into one centered on depth. This is a difficult transition, and as with many such efforts, well-reasoned, pragmatic arguments can motivate you only to a certain point. Eventually, the goal you pursue needs to resonate at a more human level. This chapter argues that when it comes to the embrace of depth, such resonance is inevitable. Whether you approach the activity of going deep from the perspective of neuroscience, psychology, or lofty philosophy, these paths all seem to lead back to a connection between depth and meaning. It's as if our species has evolved into one that flourishes in depth and wallows in shallowness, becoming what we might call *Homo sapiens deepensis*.

I earlier quoted Winifred Gallagher, the converted disciple of depth, saying, "I'll live the focused life, because it's the best kind there is." This is perhaps the best way to sum up the argument of this chapter and of Part 1 more broadly: A deep life is a good life, any way you look at it.

PART 2

The Rules

Rule #1

Work Deeply

Soon after I met David Dewane for a drink at a Dupont Circle bar, he brought up the Eudaimonia Machine. Dewane is an architecture professor, and therefore likes to explore the intersection between the conceptual and the concrete. The Eudaimonia Machine is a good example of this intersection. The machine, which takes its name from the ancient Greek concept of *eudaimonia* (a state in which you're achieving your full human potential), turns out to be a building. "The goal of the machine," David explained, "is to create a setting where the users can get into a state of deep human flourishing—creating work that's at the absolute extent of their personal abilities." It is, in other words, a space designed for the sole purpose of enabling the deepest possible deep work. I was, as you might expect, intrigued.

As Dewane explained the machine to me, he grabbed a pen to sketch its proposed layout. The structure is a one-story narrow rectangle made up of five rooms, placed in a line, one after another. There's no shared hallway: you have to pass through one room to get to the next. As Dewane explains, "[The lack of circulation] is critical because it doesn't allow you to bypass any of the spaces as you get deeper into the machine."

The first room you enter when coming off the street is called the gallery. In Dewane's plan, this room would contain examples of deep work produced in the building. It's meant to inspire users of the machine, creating a "culture of healthy stress and peer pressure."

As you leave the gallery, you next enter the salon. In here, Dewane imagines access to high-quality coffee and perhaps even a full bar. There are also couches and Wi-Fi. The salon is designed to create a mood that "hovers between intense curiosity and argumentation." This is a place to debate, "brood," and in general work through the ideas that you'll develop deeper in the machine.

Beyond the salon you enter the library. This room stores a permanent record of all work produced in the machine, as well as the books and other resources used in this previous work. There will be copiers and scanners for gathering and collecting the information you need for your project. Dewane describes the library as "the hard drive of the machine."

The next room is the office space. It contains a standard conference room with a whiteboard and some cubicles with desks. "The office," Dewane explains, "is for low-intensity activity." To use our terminology, this is the space to complete the shallow efforts required by your project. Dewane imagines an administrator with a desk in the office who could help its users improve their work habits to optimize their efficiency.

This brings us to the final room of the machine, a collection of what Dewane calls "deep work chambers" (he adopted the term "deep work" from my articles on the topic). Each chamber is conceived to be six by ten feet and protected by thick soundproof walls (Dewane's plans call for eighteen inches of insulation). "The purpose of the deep work chamber is to allow for total focus and uninterrupted work flow," Dewane explains. He imagines a process in which you spend ninety minutes inside, take a ninety-minute break, and repeat two or three times—at which point your brain will have achieved its limit of concentration for the day.

For now, the Eudaimonia Machine exists only as a collection of architectural drawings, but even as a plan, its potential to support impactful work excites Dewane. "[This design] remains, in my mind, the most interesting piece of architecture I've ever produced," he told me.

In an ideal world—one in which the true value of deep work is accepted and celebrated—we'd all have access to something like the Eudaimonia Machine. Perhaps not David Dewane's exact design, but, more generally speaking, a work environment (and culture) designed to help us extract as much value as possible from our brains. Unfortunately, this vision is far from our current reality. We instead find ourselves in distracting open offices where inboxes cannot be neglected and meetings are incessant—a setting where colleagues would rather you respond quickly to their latest e-mail than produce the best possible results. As a reader of this book, in other words, you're a disciple of depth in a shallow world.

This rule—the first of four such rules in Part 2 of this book—is designed to reduce this conflict. You might not have access to your own Eudaimonia Machine, but the strategies that follow will help you simulate its effects in your otherwise distracted professional life. They'll show you how to transform deep work from an aspiration into a regular and significant part of your daily schedule. (Rules #2 through #4 will then help you get the most out of this deep work habit by presenting, among other things, strategies for training your concentration ability and fighting back encroaching distractions.)

Before proceeding to these strategies, however, I want to first address a question that might be nagging you: Why do we need such involved interventions? Put another way, once you accept that deep work is valuable, isn't it enough to just start doing more of it? Do we really need something as complicated as the Eudaimonia Machine (or its equivalent) for something as simple as remembering to concentrate more often?

Unfortunately, when it comes to replacing distraction with focus, matters are not so simple. To understand why this is true let's take a closer look at one of the main obstacles to going deep: the urge to turn your attention toward something more superficial. Most people recognize that this urge can complicate efforts to concentrate on hard things, but most underestimate its regularity and strength.

Consider a 2012 study, led by psychologists Wilhelm Hofmann and Roy Baumeister, that outfitted 205 adults with beepers that activated at randomly selected times (this is the experience sampling method discussed in Part 1). When the beeper sounded, the subject was asked to pause for a moment to reflect on desires that he or she was currently feeling or had felt in the last thirty minutes, and then answer a set of questions about these desires. After a week, the researchers had gathered more than 7,500 samples. Here's the short version of what they found: *People fight desires all day long.* As Baumeister summarized in his subsequent book, *Willpower* (co-authored with the science writer John Tierney): "Desire turned out to be the norm, not the exception."

The five most common desires these subjects fought include, not surprisingly, eating, sleeping, and sex. But the top five list also included desires for "taking a break from [hard] work…checking e-mail and social networking sites, surfing the web, listening to music, or watching television." The lure of the Internet and television proved especially strong: The subjects succeeded in resisting these particularly addictive distractions only around half the time.

These results are bad news for this rule's goal of helping you cultivate a deep work habit. They tell us that you can expect to be bombarded with the desire to do anything *but* work deeply throughout the day, and if you're like the German subjects from the Hofmann and Baumeister study, these competing desires will often win out. You might respond at this point that *you* will succeed where these subjects failed because you understand the importance of depth and will therefore be more rigorous in your will to remain concentrated. This is a noble sentiment, but the decades of research that preceded this study underscore its futility. A now voluminous line of inquiry, initiated in a series of pioneering papers also written by Roy Baumeister, has established the following important (and at the time, unexpected) truth about willpower: *You have a finite amount of willpower that becomes depleted as you use it.*

Your will, in other words, is not a manifestation of your character that you can deploy without limit; it's instead like a muscle that tires. This is why the subjects in the Hofmann and Baumeister study had such a hard time fighting desires—over time these distractions drained their finite pool of willpower until they could no longer resist. The same will happen to you, regardless of your intentions—unless, that is, you're smart about your habits.

This brings me to the motivating idea behind the strategies that follow: The key to developing a deep work habit is to move beyond good intentions and add *routines* and *rituals* to your working life designed to minimize the amount of your limited willpower necessary to transition into and maintain a state of unbroken concentration. If you suddenly decide, for example, in the middle of a distracted afternoon spent Web browsing, to switch your attention to a cognitively demanding task, you'll draw heavily from your finite willpower to wrest your attention away from the online shininess. Such attempts will therefore frequently fail. On the other hand, if you deployed smart routines and rituals—perhaps a set time and quiet location used for your deep tasks each afternoon—you'd require much less willpower to start and keep going. In the long run, you'd therefore succeed with these deep efforts far more often.

With this in mind, the six strategies that follow can be understood as an arsenal of routines and rituals designed with the science of limited willpower in mind to maximize the amount of deep work you consistently accomplish in your schedule. Among other things, they'll ask you to commit to a particular pattern for scheduling this work and develop rituals to sharpen your concentration before starting each session. Some of these strategies will deploy simple heuristics to hijack your brain's motivation center while others are designed to recharge your willpower reserves at the fastest possible rate.

You could just try to make deep work a priority. But supporting this decision with the strategies that follow—or strategies of your own devising that are motivated by the same principles—will significantly increase the probability that you succeed in making deep work a crucial part of your professional life.

Decide on Your Depth Philosophy

The famed computer scientist Donald Knuth cares about deep work. As he explains on his website: "What I do takes long hours of studying and uninterruptible concentration." A doctoral candidate named Brian Chappell, who is a father with a full-time job, also values deep work, as it's the only way he can make progress on his dissertation given his limited time. Chappell told me that his first encounter with the idea of deep work was "an emotional moment."

I mention these examples because although Knuth and Chappell agree on the importance of depth, they disagree on their *philosophies* for integrating this depth into their work lives. As I'll detail in the next section, Knuth deploys a form of monasticism that prioritizes deep work by trying to eliminate or minimize all other types of work. Chappell, by contrast, deploys a rhythmic strategy in which he works for the same hours (five to seven thirty a.m.) every weekday morning, without exception, before beginning a workday punctuated by standard distractions. Both approaches work, but not universally. Knuth's approach might make sense for someone whose primary professional obligation is to think big thoughts, but if Chappell adopted a similar rejection of all things shallow, he'd likely lose his job.

You need your own philosophy for integrating deep work into your professional life. (As argued in this rule's introduction, attempting to schedule deep work in an ad hoc fashion is not an effective way to manage your limited willpower.) But this example highlights a general warning about this selection: You must be careful to choose a philosophy that fits your specific circumstances, as a mismatch here can derail your deep work habit before it has a chance to solidify. This strategy will help you avoid this fate by presenting four different depth philosophies that I've seen work exceptionally well in practice. The goal is to convince you that there are many different ways to integrate deep work into your schedule, and it's therefore worth taking the time to find an approach that makes sense for you.

The Monastic Philosophy of Deep Work Scheduling

Let's return to Donald Knuth. He's famous for many innovations in computer science, including, notably, the development of a rigorous approach to analyzing algorithm performance.

Among his peers, however, Knuth also maintains an aura of infamy for his approach to electronic communication. If you visit Knuth's website at Stanford with the intention of finding his e-mail address, you'll instead discover the following note:

> I have been a happy man ever since January 1, 1990, when I no longer had an email address. I'd used email since about 1975, and it seems to me that 15 years of email is plenty for one lifetime. Email is a wonderful thing for people whose role in life is to be on top of things. But not for me; my role is to be on the bottom of things. What I do takes long hours of studying and uninterruptible concentration.

Knuth goes on to acknowledge that he doesn't intend to cut himself off completely from the world. He notes that writing his books requires communication with thousands of people and that he wants to be responsive to questions and comments. His solution? He provides an address—a *postal mailing* address. He says that his administrative assistant will sort through any letters arriving at that address and put aside those that she thinks are relevant. Anything that's truly urgent she'll bring to Knuth promptly, and everything else he'll handle in a big batch, once every three months or so.

Knuth deploys what I call the *monastic philosophy* of deep work scheduling. This philosophy attempts to maximize deep efforts by eliminating or radically minimizing shallow obligations. Practitioners of the monastic philosophy tend to have a well-defined and highly valued professional goal that they're pursuing, and the bulk of their professional success comes from doing this one thing exceptionally well. It's this clarity that helps them eliminate the thicket of shallow concerns that tend to trip up those whose value proposition in the working world is more varied.

Knuth, for example, explains his professional goal as follows: "I try to learn certain areas of computer science exhaustively; then I try to digest that knowledge into a form that is accessible to people who don't have time for such study." Trying to pitch Knuth on the intangible returns of building an audience on Twitter, or the unexpected opportunities that might come through a more liberal use of e-mail, will fail, as these behaviors don't directly aid his goal to exhaustively understand specific corners of computer science and then write about them in an accessible manner.

Another person committed to monastic deep work is the acclaimed science fiction writer Neal Stephenson. If you visit Stephenson's author website, you'll notice a lack of e-mail or mailing address. We can gain insight into this omission from a pair of essays that Stephenson posted on his early website (hosted on The Well) back in the early 2000s, and which have been preserved by the Internet Archive. In one such essay, archived in 2003, Stephenson summarizes his communication policy as follows:

> *Persons who wish to interfere with my concentration are politely requested not to do so, and warned that I don't answer e-mail...lest [my communication policy's] key message get lost in the verbiage, I will put it here*

succinctly: All of my time and attention are spoken for—several times over. Please do not ask for them.

To further justify this policy, Stephenson wrote an essay titled "Why I Am a Bad Correspondent." At the core of his explanation for his inaccessibility is the following decision:

The productivity equation is a non-linear one, in other words. This accounts for why I am a bad correspondent and why I very rarely accept speaking engagements. If I organize my life in such a way that I get lots of long, consecutive, uninterrupted time-chunks, I can write novels. But as those chunks get separated and fragmented, my productivity as a novelist drops spectacularly.

Stephenson sees two mutually exclusive options: He can write good novels at a regular rate, or he can answer a lot of individual e-mails and attend conferences, and as a result produce lower-quality novels at a slower rate. He chose the former option, and this choice requires him to avoid as much as possible any source of shallow work in his professional life. (This issue is so important to Stephenson that he went on to explore its implications—positive and negative—in his 2008 science fiction epic, *Anathem*, which considers a world where an intellectual elite live in monastic orders, isolated from the distracted masses and technology, thinking deep thoughts.)

In my experience, the monastic philosophy makes many knowledge workers defensive. The clarity with which its adherents identify their value to the world, I suspect, touches a raw nerve for those whose contribution to the information economy is more complex. Notice, of course, that "more complex" does not mean "lesser." A high-level manager, for example, might play a vital role in the functioning of a billion-dollar company, even if she cannot point to something discrete, like a completed novel, and say, "This is what I produced this year." Therefore, the pool of individuals to whom the monastic philosophy applies is limited—and that's okay. If you're outside this pool, its radical simplicity shouldn't evince too much envy. On the other hand, if you're inside this pool—someone whose contribution to the world is discrete, clear, and individualized*—then you should give this philosophy serious consideration, as it might be the deciding factor between an average career and one that will be remembered.

The Bimodal Philosophy of Deep Work Scheduling

This book opened with a story about the revolutionary psychologist and thinker Carl Jung. In the 1920s, at the same time that Jung was attempting to break away from the strictures of his mentor, Sigmund Freud, he began regular retreats to a

---

* I'm being somewhat loose in my use of the word "individualized" here. The monastic philosophy does not apply *only* to those who work by themselves. There are examples of deep endeavors where the work is done among a small group. Think, for example, of songwriting teams like Rodgers and Hammerstein, or invention teams like the Wright brothers. What I really mean to indicate with my use of the term is that this philosophy applies well to those who can work toward clear goals without the other obligations that come along with being a member of a larger organization.

rustic stone house he built in the woods outside the small town of Bollingen. When there, Jung would lock himself every morning into a minimally appointed room to write without interruption. He would then meditate and walk in the woods to clarify his thinking in preparation for the next day's writing. These efforts, I argued, were aimed at increasing the intensity of Jung's deep work to a level that would allow him to succeed in intellectual combat with Freud and his many supporters.

In recalling this story I want to emphasize something important: Jung did *not* deploy a monastic approach to deep work. Donald Knuth and Neal Stephenson, our examples from earlier, attempted to completely eliminate distraction and shallowness from their professional lives. Jung, by contrast, sought this elimination only during the periods he spent at his retreat. The rest of Jung's time was spent in Zurich, where his life was anything but monastic: He ran a busy clinical practice that often had him seeing patients until late at night; he was an active participant in the Zurich coffeehouse culture; and he gave and attended many lectures in the city's respected universities. (Einstein received his doctorate from one university in Zurich and later taught at another; he also, interestingly enough, knew Jung, and the two shared several dinners to discuss the key ideas of Einstein's special relativity.) Jung's life in Zurich, in other words, is similar in many ways to the modern archetype of the hyperconnected digital-age knowledge worker: Replace "Zurich" with "San Francisco" and "letter" with "tweet" and we could be discussing some hotshot tech CEO.

Jung's approach is what I call the *bimodal philosophy* of deep work. This philosophy asks that you divide your time, dedicating some clearly defined stretches to deep pursuits and leaving the rest open to everything else. During the deep time, the bimodal worker will act monastically—seeking intense and uninterrupted concentration. During the shallow time, such focus is not prioritized. This division of time between deep and open can happen on multiple scales. For example, on the scale of a week, you might dedicate a four-day weekend to depth and the rest to open time. Similarly, on the scale of a year, you might dedicate one season to contain most of your deep stretches (as many academics do over the summer or while on sabbatical).

The bimodal philosophy believes that deep work can produce extreme productivity, *but only if* the subject dedicates enough time to such endeavors to reach maximum cognitive intensity—the state in which real breakthroughs occur. This is why the minimum unit of time for deep work in this philosophy tends to be at least one full day. To put aside a few hours in the morning, for example, is too short to count as a deep work stretch for an adherent of this approach.

At the same time, the bimodal philosophy is typically deployed by people who cannot succeed in the absence of substantial commitments to non-deep pursuits. Jung, for example, needed his clinical practice to pay the bills and the Zurich coffeehouse scene to stimulate his thinking. The approach of shifting between two modes provides a way to serve both needs well.

To provide a more modern example of the bimodal

philosophy in action, we can once again consider Adam Grant, the Wharton Business School professor whose thoughtfulness about work habits was first introduced in Part 1. As you might recall, Grant's schedule during his rapid rise through the professorship ranks at Wharton provides a nice bimodality case study. On the scale of the academic year, he stacked his courses into one semester, so that he could focus the other on deep work. During these deep semesters he then applied the bimodal approach on the weekly scale. He would, perhaps once or twice a month, take a period of two to four days to become completely monastic. He would shut his door, put an out-of-office auto-responder on his e-mail, and work on his research without interruption. Outside of these deep sessions, Grant remained famously open and accessible. In some sense, he had to be: His 2013 bestseller, *Give and Take*, promotes the practice of giving of your time and attention, without expectation of something in return, as a key strategy in professional advancement.

Those who deploy the bimodal philosophy of deep work admire the productivity of the monastics but also respect the value they receive from the shallow behaviors in their working lives. Perhaps the biggest obstacle to implementing this philosophy is that even short periods of deep work require a flexibility that many fear they lack in their current positions. If even an hour away from your inbox makes you uncomfortable, then certainly the idea of disappearing for a day or more at a time will seem impossible. But I suspect bimodal working is compatible with more types of jobs than you might guess. Earlier, for example, I described a study by Harvard Business School professor Leslie Perlow. In this study, a group of management consultants were asked to disconnect for a full day each workweek. The consultants were afraid the client would rebel. It turned out that the client didn't care. As Jung, Grant, and Perlow's subjects discovered, people will usually respect your right to become inaccessible if these periods are well defined and well advertised, and outside these stretches, you're once again easy to find.

The Rhythmic Philosophy of
Deep Work Scheduling

In the early days of the *Seinfeld* show, Jerry Seinfeld remained a working comic with a busy tour schedule. It was during this period that a writer and comic named Brad Isaac, who was working open mic nights at the time, ran into Seinfeld at a club waiting to go on stage. As Isaac later explained in a now classic Lifehacker article: "I saw my chance. I had to ask Seinfeld if he had any tips for a young comic. What he told me was something that would benefit me for a lifetime."

Seinfeld began his advice to Isaac with some common sense, noting "the way to be a better comic was to create better jokes," and then explaining that the way to create better jokes was to write every day. Seinfeld continued by describing a specific technique he used to help maintain this discipline. He keeps a calendar on his wall. Every day that he writes jokes he crosses out the date on the calendar with a big red *X*. "After a few days you'll have a chain," Seinfeld said. "Just keep at it and the chain will grow longer every day. You'll like seeing that chain, especially when you get a few weeks under your belt. Your only job next is to not break the chain."

This *chain method* (as some now call it) soon became a hit among writers and fitness enthusiasts—communities that thrive on the ability to do hard things consistently. For our purposes, it provides a specific example of a general approach to integrating depth into your life: the *rhythmic philosophy*. This philosophy argues that the easiest way to consistently start deep work sessions is to transform them into a simple regular habit. The goal, in other words, is to generate a *rhythm* for this work that removes the need for you to invest energy in deciding if and when you're going to go deep. The chain method is a good example of the rhythmic philosophy of deep work scheduling because it combines a simple scheduling heuristic (do the work every day), with an easy way to remind yourself to do the work: the big red *X*s on the calendar.

Another common way to implement the rhythmic philosophy is to replace the visual aid of the chain method with a set starting time that you use every day for deep work. In much the same way that maintaining visual indicators of your work progress can reduce the barrier to entry for going deep, eliminating even the simplest scheduling decisions, such as when during the day to do the work, also reduces this barrier.

Consider the example of Brian Chappell, the busy doctoral candidate I introduced in the opening to this strategy. Chappell adopted the rhythmic philosophy of deep work scheduling out of necessity. Around the time that he was ramping up his dissertation writing he was offered a full-time job at a center on the campus where he was a student. Professionally, this was a good opportunity and Chappell was happy to accept it. But academically, a full-time job, especially when coupled with the recent arrival of Chappell's first child, made it difficult to find the depth needed to write thesis chapters.

Chappell began by attempting a vague commitment to deep work. He made a rule that deep work needed to happen in ninety-minute chunks (recognizing correctly that it takes time to ease into a state of concentration) and he decided he would try to schedule these chunks in an ad hoc manner whenever appropriate openings in his schedule arose. Not surprisingly, this strategy didn't yield much productivity. In a dissertation boot camp Chappell had attended the year before, he'd managed to produce a full thesis chapter in a single week of rigorous deep work. After he accepted his full-time job, he managed to produce only a single additional chapter in *the entire first year* he was working.

It was the glacial writing progress during this year that drove Chappell to embrace the rhythmic method. He made a rule that he would wake up and start working by five thirty every morning. He would then work until seven thirty, make breakfast, and go to work already done with his dissertation obligations for the day. Pleased by early progress, he soon pushed his wake-up time to four forty-five to squeeze out even more morning depth.

When I interviewed Chappell for this book, he described his rhythmic approach to deep work scheduling as "both astronomically productive and guilt free." His routine was producing four to five pages of academic prose per day and was capable of generating drafts of thesis chapters at a rate of one chapter *every two or three weeks*: a phenomenal output for someone who also worked a nine-to-five job. "Who's to say that I can't be that prolific?" he concluded. "Why not me?"

The rhythmic philosophy provides an interesting contrast to the bimodal philosophy. It perhaps fails to achieve the most intense levels of deep thinking sought in the day-long concentration sessions favored by the bimodalist. The trade-off, however, is that this approach works better with the reality of human nature. By supporting deep work with rock-solid routines that make sure a little bit gets done on a regular basis, the rhythmic scheduler will often log a larger total number of deep hours per year.

The decision between rhythmic and bimodal can come down to your self-control in such scheduling matters. If you're Carl Jung and are engaged in an intellectual dogfight with Sigmund Freud's supporters, you'll likely have no trouble recognizing the importance of finding time to focus on your ideas. On the other hand, if you're writing a dissertation with no one pressuring you to get it done, the habitual nature of the rhythmic philosophy might be necessary to maintain progress.

For many, however, it's not just self-control issues that bias them toward the rhythmic philosophy, but also the reality that some jobs don't allow you to disappear for days at a time when the need to go deep arises. (For a lot of bosses, the standard is that you're free to focus as hard as you want...so long as the boss's e-mails are still answered promptly.) This is likely the biggest reason why the rhythmic philosophy is one of the most common among deep workers in standard office jobs.

The Journalistic Philosophy of Deep Work Scheduling

In the 1980s, the journalist Walter Isaacson was in his thirties and well along in his rapid ascent through the ranks of *Time* magazine. By this point, he was undoubtedly on the radar of the thinking class. Christopher Hitchens, for example, writing in the *London Review of Books* during this period, called him "one of the best magazine journalists in America." The time was right for Isaacson to write a Big Important Book—a necessary step on the ladder of journalistic achievement. So Isaacson chose a complicated topic, an intertwined narrative biography of six figures who played an important role in early Cold War policy, and teamed up with a fellow young *Time* editor, Evan Thomas, to produce an appropriately weighty book: an 864-page epic titled *The Wise Men: Six Friends and the World They Made*.

This book, which was published in 1986, was well received by the right people. The *New York Times* called it "a richly textured account," while the *San Francisco Chronicle* exulted that the two young writers had "fashioned a Cold War Plutarch." Less than a decade later, Isaacson reached the apex of his journalism career when he was appointed editor of *Time* (which he then followed with a second act as the CEO of a think tank and an incredibly popular biographer of figures including Benjamin Franklin, Albert Einstein, and Steve Jobs).

What interests me about Isaacson, however, is not *what* he accomplished with his first book but *how* he wrote it. In uncovering this story, I must draw from a fortunate personal connection. As it turns out, in the years leading up to the publication of *The Wise Men*, my uncle John Paul Newport, who was also a journalist in New York at the time, shared a summer beach rental with Isaacson. To this day, my uncle remembers Isaacson's impressive work habits:

> *It was always amazing… he could retreat up to the bedroom for a while, when the rest of us were chilling on the patio or whatever, to work on his book… he'd go up for twenty minutes or an hour, we'd hear the typewriter pounding, then he'd come down as relaxed as the rest of us… the work never seemed to faze him, he just happily went up to work when he had the spare time.*

Isaacson was methodic: Any time he could find some free time, he would switch into a deep work mode and hammer away at his book. This is how, it turns out, one can write a nine-hundred-page book on the side while spending the bulk of one's day becoming one of the country's best magazine writers.

I call this approach, in which you fit deep work wherever you can into your schedule, the *journalist philosophy*. This name is a nod to the fact that journalists, like Walter Isaacson, are trained to shift into a writing mode on a moment's notice, as is required by the deadline-driven nature of their profession.

This approach is not for the deep work novice. As I established in the opening to this rule, the ability to rapidly switch your mind from shallow to deep mode doesn't come naturally. Without practice, such switches can seriously deplete your finite willpower reserves. This habit also requires a sense of confidence in your abilities—a conviction that what you're doing is important and will succeed. This type of conviction is typically built on a foundation of existing professional accomplishment. Isaacson, for example, likely had an easier time switching to writing mode than, say, a first-time novelist, because Isaacson had worked himself up to become a respected writer by this point. He *knew* he had the capacity to write an epic biography and understood it to be a key task in his professional advancement. This confidence goes a long way in motivating hard efforts.

I'm partial to the journalistic philosophy of deep work because it's my main approach to integrating these efforts into my schedule. In other words, I'm not monastic in my deep work (though I do find myself occasionally jealous of my fellow computer scientist Donald Knuth's unapologetic disconnection), I don't deploy multiday depth binges like the bimodalists, and though I am intrigued by the rhythmic philosophy, my schedule has a way of thwarting attempts to enforce a daily habit. Instead, in an ode to Isaacson, I face each week as it arrives and do my best to squeeze out as much depth as possible. To write this book, for example, I had to take advantage of free stretches of time wherever they popped up. If my kids were taking a good nap, I'd grab my laptop and lock myself in the home office. If my wife wanted to visit her parents in nearby Annapolis on a weekend day, I'd take advantage of the extra child care to disappear to a quiet corner of their house to write. If a meeting at work was canceled, or an afternoon left open, I might retreat to one of my favorite libraries on campus to squeeze out a few hundred more words. And so on.

I should admit that I'm not pure in my application of the journalist philosophy. I don't, for example, make all my deep work decisions on a moment-to-moment basis. I instead tend to map out when I'll work deeply during each week at the beginning of the week, and then refine these decisions, as needed, at the beginning of each day (see Rule #4 for more details on my scheduling routines). By reducing the need to make decisions about deep work moment by moment, I can preserve more mental energy for the deep thinking itself.

In the final accounting, the journalistic philosophy of deep work scheduling remains difficult to pull off. But if you're confident in the value of what you're trying to produce, and practiced in the skill of going deep (a skill we will continue to develop in the strategies that follow), it can be a surprisingly robust way to squeeze out large amounts of depth from an otherwise demanding schedule.

Ritualize

An often-overlooked observation about those who use their minds to create valuable things is that they're rarely haphazard in their work habits. Consider the Pulitzer Prize–winning biographer Robert Caro. As revealed in a 2009 magazine profile, "every inch of [Caro's] New York office is governed by rules." Where he places his books, how he stacks his notebooks, what he puts on his wall, even what he wears to the office: Everything is specified by a routine that has varied little over Caro's long career. "I trained myself to be organized," he explained.

Charles Darwin had a similarly strict structure for his working life during the period when he was perfecting *On the Origin of Species*. As his son Francis later remembered, he would rise promptly at seven to take a short walk. He would then eat breakfast alone and retire to his study from eight to nine thirty. The next hour was dedicated to reading his letters from the day before, after which he would return to his study from ten thirty until noon. After this session, he would mull over challenging ideas while walking on a proscribed route that started at his greenhouse and then circled a path on his property. He would walk until satisfied with his thinking then declare his workday done.

The journalist Mason Currey, who spent half a decade cataloging the habits of famous thinkers and writers (and from whom I learned the previous two examples), summarized this tendency toward systematization as follows:

> *There is a popular notion that artists work from inspiration—that there is some strike or bolt or bubbling up of creative mojo from who knows where . . . but I hope [my work] makes clear that waiting for inspiration to strike is a terrible, terrible plan. In fact, perhaps*

the single best piece of advice I can offer to anyone try-ing to do creative work is to ignore inspiration.

In a *New York Times* column on the topic, David Brooks summarizes this reality more bluntly: "[Great creative minds] think like artists but work like accountants."

This strategy suggests the following: To make the most out of your deep work sessions, build rituals of the same level of strictness and idiosyncrasy as the important thinkers mentioned previously. There's a good reason for this mimicry. Great minds like Caro and Darwin didn't deploy rituals to be weird; they did so because success in their work depended on their ability to go deep, again and again—there's no way to win a Pulitzer Prize or conceive a grand theory without pushing your brain to its limit. Their rituals minimized the friction in this transition to depth, allowing them to go deep more easily and stay in the state longer. If they had instead waited for inspiration to strike before settling in to serious work, their accomplishments would likely have been greatly reduced.

There's no one *correct* deep work ritual—the right fit depends on both the person and the type of project pursued. But there are some general questions that any effective ritual must address:

- **Where you'll work and for how long**. Your ritual needs to specify a location for your deep work efforts. This location can be as simple as your normal office with the door shut and desk cleaned off (a colleague of mine likes to put a hotel-style "do not disturb" sign on his office door when he's tackling something difficult). If it's possible to identify a location used *only* for depth—for instance, a conference room or quiet library—the positive effect can be even greater. (If you work in an open office plan, this need to find a deep work retreat becomes particularly important.) Regardless of where you work, be sure to also give yourself a specific time frame to keep the session a discrete challenge and not an open-ended slog.

- **How you'll work once you start to work**. Your ritual needs rules and processes to keep your efforts structured. For example, you might institute a ban on any Internet use, or maintain a metric such as words produced per twenty-minute interval to keep your concentration honed. Without this structure, you'll have to mentally litigate again and again what you should and should not be doing during these sessions and keep trying to assess whether you're working sufficiently hard. These are unnecessary drains on your willpower reserves.

- **How you'll support your work**. Your ritual needs to ensure your brain gets the support it needs to keep operating at a high level of depth. For example, the ritual might specify that you start with a cup of good coffee, or make sure you have access to enough food of the right type to maintain energy, or integrate light exercise such as walking to help keep the mind clear. (As Nietzsche said: "It is only ideas gained from walking that have any worth.") This support might also include environmental factors, such as organizing the raw materials of your work to minimize energy-dissipating friction (as we saw with Caro's example). To maximize your success, you need to support your efforts to go deep. At the same time, this support needs to be systematized so that you don't waste mental energy figuring out what you need in the moment.

These questions will help you get started in crafting your deep work ritual. But keep in mind that finding a ritual that sticks might require experimentation, so be willing to work at it. I assure you that the effort's worth it: Once you've evolved something that feels right, the impact can be significant. To work deeply is a big deal and should not be an activity undertaken lightly. Surrounding such efforts with a complicated (and perhaps, to the outside world, quite strange) ritual accepts this reality—providing your mind with the structure and commitment it needs to slip into the state of focus where you can begin to create things that matter.

Make Grand Gestures

In the early winter of 2007, J.K. Rowling was struggling to complete *The Deathly Hallows*, the final book in her Harry Potter series. The pressure was intense, as this book bore the responsibility of tying together the six that preceded it in a way that would satisfy the series' hundreds of millions of fans. Rowling needed to work deeply to satisfy these demands, but she was finding unbroken concentration increasingly difficult to achieve at her home office in Edinburgh, Scotland. "As I was finishing *Deathly Hallows* there came a day where the window cleaner came, the kids were at home, the dogs were barking," Rowling recalled in an interview. It was too much, so J.K. Rowling decided to do something extreme to shift her mind-set where it needed to be: She checked into a suite in the five-star Balmoral Hotel, located in the heart of downtown Edinburgh. "So I came to this hotel because it's a beautiful hotel, but I didn't intend to stay here," she explained. "[But] the first day's writing went well so I kept coming back... and I ended up finishing the last of the *Harry Potter* books [here]."

In retrospect, it's not surprising that Rowling ended up staying. The setting was perfect for her project. The Balmoral, known as one of Scotland's most luxurious hotels, is a classic Victorian building complete with ornate stonework and a tall clock tower. It's also located only a couple of blocks away from Edinburgh Castle—one of Rowling's inspirations in dreaming up Hogwarts.

Rowling's decision to check into a luxurious hotel suite near Edinburgh Castle is an example of a curious but effective strategy in the world of deep work: *the grand gesture*. The concept is simple: By leveraging a radical change to your normal environment, coupled perhaps with a significant investment of effort or money, all dedicated toward supporting a deep work task, you increase the perceived importance of the task. This boost in importance reduces your mind's instinct to procrastinate and delivers an injection of motivation and energy.

Writing a chapter of a Harry Potter novel, for example, is hard work and will require a lot of mental energy—regardless of where you do it. But when paying more than $1,000 a day to write the chapter in a suite of an old hotel down the street from a Hogwarts-style castle, *mustering* the energy to begin and sustain this work is easier than if you were instead in a distracting home office.

When you study the habits of other well-known deep workers, the grand gesture strategy comes up often. Bill Gates, for example, was famous during his time as Microsoft CEO for taking Think Weeks during which he would leave behind his normal work and family obligations to retreat to a cabin with a stack of papers and books. His goal was to think deeply, without distraction, about the big issues relevant to his company. It was during one of these weeks, for example, that he famously came to the conclusion that the Internet was going to be a major force in the industry. There was nothing physically stopping Gates from thinking deeply in his office in Microsoft's Seattle headquarters, but the novelty of his weeklong retreat helped him achieve the desired levels of concentration.

The MIT physicist and award-winning novelist Alan Lightman also leverages grand gestures. In his case, he retreats each summer to a "tiny island" in Maine to think deeply and recharge. At least as of 2000, when he described this gesture in an interview, the island not only lacked Internet, but didn't even have phone service. As he then justified:

"It's really about two and a half months that I'll feel like I can recover some silence in my life . . . which is so hard to find."

Not everyone has the freedom to spend two months in Maine, but many writers, including Dan Pink and Michael Pollan, simulate the experience year-round by building—often at significant expense and effort—writing cabins on their properties. (Pollan, for his part, even wrote a book about his experience building his cabin in the woods behind his former Connecticut home.) These outbuildings aren't strictly necessary for these writers, who need only a laptop and a flat surface to put it on to ply their trade. But it's not the amenities of the cabins that generate their value; it's instead the grand gesture represented in the design and building of the cabin for the sole purpose of enabling better writing.

Not every grand gesture need be so permanent. After the pathologically competitive Bell Labs physicist William Shockley was scooped in the invention of the transistor—as I detail in the next strategy, two members of his team made the breakthrough at a time when Shockley was away working on another project—he locked himself in a hotel room in Chicago, where he had traveled ostensibly to attend a conference. He didn't emerge from the room until he had ironed out the details for a better design that had been rattling around in his mind. When he finally did leave the room, he airmailed his notes back to Murray Hill, New Jersey, so that a colleague could paste them into his lab notebook and sign them to timestamp the innovation. The junction form of the transistor that Shockley worked out in this burst of depth ended up earning him a share of the Nobel Prize subsequently awarded for the invention.

An even more extreme example of a onetime grand gesture yielding results is a story involving Peter Shankman, an entrepreneur and social media pioneer. As a popular speaker, Shankman spends much of his time flying. He eventually realized that thirty thousand feet was an ideal environment for him to focus. As he explained in a blog post, "Locked in a seat with nothing in front of me, nothing to distract me, nothing to set off my 'Ooh! Shiny!' DNA, I have nothing to do but be at one with my thoughts." It was sometime after this realization that Shankman signed a book contract that gave him only two weeks to finish the entire manuscript. Meeting this deadline would require incredible concentration. To achieve this state, Shankman did something unconventional. He booked a round-trip business-class ticket to Tokyo. He wrote during the whole flight to Japan, drank an espresso in the business class lounge once he arrived in Japan, then turned around and flew back, once again writing the whole way—arriving back in the States only thirty hours after he first left with a completed manuscript now in hand. "The trip cost $4,000 and was worth every penny," he explained.

In all of these examples, it's not just the change of environment or seeking of quiet that enables more depth. The dominant force is the psychology of committing so seriously to the task at hand. To put yourself in an exotic location to focus on a writing project, or to take a week off from work just to think, or to lock yourself in a hotel room until you complete an important invention: These gestures push your deep goal to a level of mental priority that helps unlock the needed mental resources. Sometimes to go deep, you must first go big.

Don't Work Alone

The relationship between deep work and collaboration is tricky. It's worth taking the time to untangle, however, because properly leveraging collaboration can increase the quality of deep work in your professional life.

It's helpful to start our discussion of this topic by taking a step back to consider what at first seems to be an unresolvable conflict. In Part 1 of this book I criticized Facebook for the design of its new headquarters. In particular, I noted that the company's goal to create the world's largest open office space—a giant room that will reportedly hold twenty-eight hundred workers—represents an absurd attack on concentration. Both intuition and a growing body of research underscore the reality that sharing a workspace with a large number of coworkers is incredibly distracting—creating an environment that thwarts attempts to think seriously. In a 2013 article summarizing recent research on this topic, *Bloomberg Businessweek* went so far as to call for an end to the "tyranny of the open-plan office."

And yet, these open office designs are not embraced haphazardly. As Maria Konnikova reports in *The New Yorker*, when this concept first emerged, its goal was to "facilitate communication and idea flow." This claim resonated with

American businesses looking to embrace an aura of start-up unconventionality. Josh Tyrangiel, the editor of *Bloomberg Businessweek*, for example, explained the lack of offices in Bloomberg's headquarters as follows: "Open plan is pretty spectacular; it ensures that everyone is attuned to the broad mission, and...it encourages curiosity between people who work in different disciplines." Jack Dorsey justified the open layout of the Square headquarters by explaining: "We encourage people to stay out in the open because we believe in serendipity—and people walking by each other teaching new things."

For the sake of discussion, let's call this principle—that when you allow people to bump into each other smart collaborations and new ideas emerge—the *theory of serendipitous creativity*. When Mark Zuckerberg decided to build the world's largest office, we can reasonably conjecture, this theory helped drive his decision, just as it has driven many of the moves toward open workspaces elsewhere in Silicon Valley and beyond. (Other less-exalted factors, like saving money and increasing supervision, also play a role, but they're not as sexy and are therefore less emphasized.)

This decision between promoting concentration and promoting serendipity seems to indicate that deep work (an individual endeavor) is incompatible with generating creative insights (a collaborative endeavor). This conclusion, however, is flawed. It's based, I argue, on an incomplete understanding of the theory of serendipitous creativity. To support this claim, let's consider the origins of this particular understanding of what spurs breakthroughs.

The theory in question has many sources, but I happen to have a personal connection to one of the more well-known. During my seven years at MIT, I worked on the site of the institute's famed Building 20. This structure, located at the intersection of Main and Vassar Streets in East Cambridge, and eventually demolished in 1998, was thrown together as a temporary shelter during World War II, meant to house the overflow from the school's bustling Radiation Laboratory. As noted by a 2012 *New Yorker* article, the building was initially seen as a failure: "Ventilation was poor and hallways were dim. The walls were thin, the roof leaked, and the building was broiling in the summer and freezing in the winter."

When the war ended, however, the influx of scientists to Cambridge continued. MIT needed space, so instead of immediately demolishing Building 20 as they had promised local officials (in exchange for lax permitting), they continued using it as overflow space. The result was that a mismatch of different departments—from nuclear science to linguistics to electronics—shared the low-slung building alongside more esoteric tenants such as a machine shop and a piano repair facility. Because the building was cheaply constructed, these groups felt free to rearrange space as needed. Walls and floors could be shifted and equipment bolted to the beams. In recounting the story of Jerrold Zacharias's work on the first atomic clock, the abovementioned *New Yorker* article points to the importance of his ability to remove two floors from his Building 20 lab so he could install the three-story cylinder needed for his experimental apparatus.

In MIT lore, it's generally believed that this haphazard

combination of different disciplines, thrown together in a large reconfigurable building, led to chance encounters and a spirit of inventiveness that generated breakthroughs at a fast pace, innovating topics as diverse as Chomsky grammars, Loran navigational radars, and video games, all within the same productive postwar decades. When the building was finally demolished to make way for the $300 million Frank Gehry–designed Stata Center (where I spent my time), its loss was mourned. In tribute to the "plywood palace" it replaced, the interior design of the Stata Center includes boards of unfinished plywood and exposed concrete with construction markings left intact.

Around the same time that Building 20 was hastily constructed, a more systematic pursuit of serendipitous creativity was under way two hundred miles to the southwest in Murray Hill, New Jersey. It was here that Bell Labs director Mervin Kelly guided the construction of a new home for the lab that would purposefully encourage interaction between its diverse mix of scientists and engineers. Kelly dismissed the standard university-style approach of housing different departments in different buildings, and instead connected the spaces into one contiguous structure joined by long hallways—some so long that when you stood at one end it would appear to converge to a vanishing point. As Bell Labs chronicler Jon Gertner notes about this design: "Traveling the hall's length without encountering a number of acquaintances, problems, diversions and ideas was almost impossible. A physicist on his way to lunch in the cafeteria was like a magnet rolling past iron filings."

This strategy, mixed with Kelly's aggressive recruitment of some of the world's best minds, yielded some of the most concentrated innovation in the history of modern civilization. In the decades following the Second World War, the lab produced, among other achievements: the first solar cell, laser, communication satellite, cellular communication system, and fiber optic networking. At the same time, their theorists formulated both information theory and coding theory, their astronomers won the Nobel Prize for empirically validating the Big Bang Theory, and perhaps most important of all, their physicists invented the transistor.

The theory of serendipitous creativity, in other words, seems well justified by the historical record. The transistor, we can argue with some confidence, probably required Bell Labs and its ability to put solid-state physicists, quantum theorists, and world-class experimentalists in one building where they could serendipitously encounter one another and learn from their varied expertise. This was an invention unlikely to come from a lone scientist thinking deeply in the academic equivalent of Carl Jung's stone tower.

But it's here that we must embrace more nuance in understanding what *really* generated innovation in sites such as Building 20 and Bell Labs. To do so, let's return once again to my own experience at MIT. When I arrived as a new PhD student in the fall of 2004, I was a member of the first incoming class to be housed in the new Stata Center, which, as mentioned, replaced Building 20. Because the center was new, incoming students were given tours that touted its features. Frank Gehry, we learned, arranged the offices around common spaces and introduced open stair-wells between adjacent floors, all in an effort to support the type of serendipitous encounters that had defined its prede-cessor. But what struck me at the time was a feature that hadn't occurred to Gehry but had been recently added at the faculty's insistence: special gaskets installed into the office doorjambs to improve soundproofing. The profes-sors at MIT—some of the most innovative technologists in the world—wanted nothing to do with an open-office-style workspace. They instead demanded the ability to close themselves off.

This combination of soundproofed offices connected to large common areas yields a *hub-and-spoke* architecture of innovation in which both serendipitous encounter and iso-lated deep thinking are supported. It's a setup that straddles a spectrum where on one extreme we find the solo thinker, isolated from inspiration but free from distraction, and on the other extreme, we find the fully collaborative thinker in an open office, flush with inspiration but struggling to sup-port the deep thinking needed to build on it.*

If we turn our attention back to Building 20 and Bell Labs, we see that this is the architecture they deployed as

---

* Supporters of open office plans might claim that they're approximating this mix of depth and interaction by making available conference rooms that people can use as needed to dive deeper into an idea. This conceit, however, trivializes the role of deep work in innovation. These efforts are not an occasional accompaniment to inspirational chance encoun-ters; they instead represent the bulk of the effort involved in most real breakthroughs.

well. Neither building offered anything resembling a modern open office plan. They were instead constructed using the standard layout of private offices connected to shared hallways. Their creative mojo had more to do with the fact that these offices shared a small number of long connecting spaces—forcing researchers to interact whenever they needed to travel from one location to another. These megahallways, in other words, provided highly effective hubs.

We can, therefore, still dismiss the depth-destroying open office concept without dismissing the innovation-producing theory of serendipitous creativity. The key is to maintain both in a hub-and-spoke-style arrangement: Expose yourself to ideas in hubs on a regular basis, but maintain a spoke in which to work deeply on what you encounter.

This division of efforts, however, is not the full story, as even when one returns to a spoke, solo work is still not necessarily the best strategy. Consider, for example, the previously mentioned invention of the (point-contact) transistor at Bell Labs. This breakthrough was supported by a large group of researchers, all with separate specialties, who came together to form the *solid-state physics research group*—a team dedicated to inventing a smaller and more reliable alternative to the vacuum tube. This group's collaborative conversations were necessary preconditions to the transistor: a clear example of the usefulness of hub behavior.

Once the research group laid the intellectual groundwork for the component, the innovation process shifted to a spoke. What makes this particular innovation process an interesting case, however, is that even when it shifted to a spoke it remained collaborative. It was two researchers in particular—the experimentalist Walter Brattain and the quantum theorist John Bardeen—who over a period of one month in 1947 made the series of breakthroughs that led to the first working solid-state transistor.

Brattain and Bardeen worked together during this period in a small lab, often side by side, pushing each other toward better and more effective designs. These efforts consisted primarily of deep work—but a type of deep work we haven't yet encountered. Brattain would concentrate intensely to engineer an experimental design that could exploit Bardeen's latest theoretical insight; then Bardeen would concentrate intensely to make sense of what Brattain's latest experiments revealed, trying to expand his theoretical framework to match the observations. This back-and-forth represents a collaborative form of deep work (common in academic circles) that leverages what I call *the whiteboard effect*. For some types of problems, working with someone else at the proverbial shared whiteboard can push you deeper than if you were working alone. The presence of the other party waiting for your next insight—be it someone physically in the same room or collaborating with you virtually—can short-circuit the natural instinct to avoid depth.

We can now step back and draw some practical conclusions about the role of collaboration in deep work. The success of Building 20 and Bell Labs indicates that isolation is not required for productive deep work. Indeed, their example indicates that for many types of work—especially when pursuing innovation—collaborative deep work can yield better results. This strategy, therefore, asks that you consider this option in contemplating how best to integrate depth into your professional life. In doing so, however, keep the following two guidelines in mind.

First, distraction remains a destroyer of depth. Therefore, the hub-and-spoke model provides a crucial template. Separate your pursuit of serendipitous encounters from your efforts to think deeply and build on these inspirations. You should try to optimize each effort separately, as opposed to mixing them together into a sludge that impedes both goals.

Second, even when you retreat to a spoke to think deeply, when it's reasonable to leverage the whiteboard effect, do so. By working side by side with someone on a problem, you can push each other toward deeper levels of depth, and therefore toward the generation of more and more valuable output as compared to working alone.

When it comes to deep work, in other words, consider the use of collaboration when appropriate, as it can push your results to a new level. At the same time, don't lionize this quest for interaction and positive randomness to the point where it crowds out the unbroken concentration ultimately required to wring something useful out of the swirl of ideas all around us.

Execute Like a Business

The story has become lore in the world of business consulting. In the mid-1990s, Harvard Business School professor Clayton Christensen received a call from Andy Grove, the

CEO and chairman of Intel. Grove had encountered Christensen's research on disruptive innovation and asked him to fly out to California to discuss the theory's implications for Intel. On arrival, Christensen walked through the basics of disruption: entrenched companies are often unexpectedly dethroned by start-ups that begin with cheap offerings at the low end of the market, but then, over time, improve their cheap products *just enough* to begin to steal high-end market share. Grove recognized that Intel faced this threat from low-end processors produced by upstart companies like AMD and Cyrix. Fueled by his newfound understanding of disruption, Grove devised the strategy that led to the Celeron family of processors—a lower-performance offering that helped Intel successfully fight off the challenges from below.

There is, however, a lesser-known piece to this story. As Christensen recalls, Grove asked him during a break in this meeting, "How do I do this?" Christensen responded with a discussion of business strategy, explaining how Grove could set up a new business unit and so on. Grove cut him off with a gruff reply: "You are such a naïve academic. I asked you *how* to do it, and you told me *what* I should do. *I know what I need to do. I just don't know how to do it.*"

As Christensen later explained, this division between *what* and *how* is crucial but is overlooked in the professional world. It's often straightforward to identify a strategy needed to achieve a goal, but what trips up companies is figuring out how to execute the strategy once identified. I came across this story in a foreword Christensen wrote for a book titled

The 4 Disciplines of Execution, which built on extensive consulting case studies to describe four "disciplines" (abbreviated, 4DX) for helping companies successfully implement high-level strategies. What struck me as I read was that this gap between *what* and *how* was relevant to my personal quest to spend more time working deeply. Just as Andy Grove had identified the importance of competing in the low-end processor market, I had identified the importance of prioritizing depth. What I needed was help figuring out how to execute this strategy.

Intrigued by these parallels, I set out to adapt the 4DX framework to my personal work habits and ended up surprised by how helpful they proved in driving me toward effective action on my goal of working deeply. These ideas may have been forged for the world of big business, but the underlying concepts seem to apply anywhere that something important needs to get done against the backdrop of many competing obligations and distractions. With this in mind, I've summarized in the following sections the four disciplines of the 4DX framework, and for each I describe how I adapted it to the specific concerns of developing a deep work habit.

Discipline #1: *Focus on the Wildly Important*

As the authors of *The 4 Disciplines of Execution* explain, "The more you try to do, the less you actually accomplish." They elaborate that execution should be aimed at a small number of "wildly important goals." This simplicity will help focus an organization's energy to a sufficient intensity to ignite real results.

For an individual focused on deep work, the implication is that you should identify a small number of ambitious outcomes to pursue with your deep work hours. The general exhortation to "spend more time working deeply" doesn't spark a lot of enthusiasm. To instead have a specific goal that would return tangible and substantial professional benefits will generate a steadier stream of enthusiasm. In a 2014 column titled "The Art of Focus," David Brooks endorsed this approach of letting ambitious goals drive focused behavior, explaining: "If you want to win the war for attention, don't try to say 'no' to the trivial distractions you find on the information smorgasbord; try to say 'yes' to the subject that arouses a terrifying longing, and let the terrifying longing crowd out everything else."

For example, when I first began experimenting with 4DX, I set the specific important goal of publishing five high-quality peer-reviewed papers in the upcoming academic year. This goal was ambitious, as it was more papers than I had been publishing, and there were tangible rewards attached to it (tenure review was looming). Combined, these two properties helped the goal stoke my motivation.

Discipline #2: Act on the Lead Measures

Once you've identified a wildly important goal, you need to measure your success. In 4DX, there are two types of metrics for this purpose: *lag* measures and *lead* measures. Lag measures describe the thing you're ultimately trying to improve. For example, if your goal is to increase customer satisfaction in your bakery, then the relevant lag measure is your customer satisfaction scores. As the 4DX authors explain, the problem with lag measures is that they come too late to change your behavior: "When you receive them, the performance that drove them is already in the past."

Lead measures, on the other hand, "measure the new behaviors that will drive success on the lag measures." In the bakery example, a good lead measure might be the number of customers who receive free samples. This is a number you can directly increase by giving out more samples. As you increase this number, your lag measures will likely eventually improve as well. In other words, lead measures turn your attention to improving the behaviors you directly control in the near future that will then have a positive impact on your long-term goals.

For an individual focused on deep work, it's easy to identify the relevant lead measure: *time spent in a state of deep work dedicated toward your wildly important goal.* Returning to my example, this insight had an important impact on how I directed my academic research. I used to focus on lag measures, such as papers published per year. These measures, however, lacked influence on my day-to-day behavior because there was nothing I could do in the short term that could immediately generate a noticeable change to this long-term metric. When I shifted to tracking deep work hours, suddenly these measures became relevant to my day-to-day: Every hour extra of deep work was immediately reflected in my tally.

Discipline #3: *Keep a Compelling Scoreboard*

"People play differently when they're keeping score," the 4DX authors explain. They then elaborate that when attempting to drive your team's engagement toward your organization's wildly important goal, it's important that they have a public place to record and track their lead measures. This scoreboard creates a sense of competition that drives them to focus on these measures, even when other demands vie for their attention. It also provides a reinforcing source of motivation. Once the team notices their success with a lead measure, they become invested in perpetuating this performance.

In the preceding discipline, I argued that for an individual focused on deep work, hours spent working deeply should be the lead measure. It follows, therefore, that the individual's scoreboard should be a physical artifact in the workspace that displays the individual's current deep work hour count.

In my early experiments with 4DX, I settled on a simple but effective solution for implementing this scoreboard. I took a piece of card stock and divided it into rows, one for each week of the current semester. I then labeled each row with the dates of the week and taped it to the wall next to my computer monitor (where it couldn't be ignored). As each week progressed, I kept track of the hours spent in deep work that week with a simple tally of tick marks in that week's row. To maximize the motivation generated by this scoreboard, whenever I reached an important milestone in an academic paper (e.g., solving a key proof), I would circle the tally mark corresponding to the hour where I finished the result.* This served two purposes. First, it allowed me to connect, at a visceral level, accumulated deep work hours and tangible results. Second, it helped calibrate my expectations for how many hours of deep work were needed per result. This reality (which was larger than I first assumed) helped spur me to squeeze more such hours into each week.

Discipline #4: Create a Cadence of Accountability

The 4DX authors elaborate that the final step to help maintain a focus on lead measures is to put in place "a rhythm of regular and frequent meetings of any team that owns a wildly important goal." During these meetings, the team members must confront their scoreboard, commit to specific actions to help improve the score before the next meeting, and describe what happened with the commitments they made at the last meeting. They note that this review can be condensed to only a few minutes, but it must be regular for its effect to be felt. The authors argue that it's this discipline where "execution really happens."

For an individual focused on his or her own deep work habit, there's likely no team to meet with, but this doesn't exempt you from the need for regular accountability. In

---

* You can see a snapshot of my "hour tally" online: "Deep Habits: Should You Track Hours or Milestones?" March 23, 2014, http://calnewport.com/blog/2014/03/23/deep-habits-should-you-track-hours-or-milestones/.

multiple places throughout this book I discuss and recommend the habit of a weekly review in which you make a plan for the workweek ahead (see Rule #4). During my experiments with 4DX, I used a weekly review to look over my scoreboard to celebrate good weeks, help understand what led to bad weeks, and most important, figure out how to ensure a good score for the days ahead. This led me to adjust my schedule to meet the needs of my lead measure—enabling significantly more deep work than if I had avoided such reviews altogether.

The 4DX framework is based on the fundamental premise that execution is more difficult than strategizing. After hundreds and hundreds of case studies, its inventors managed to isolate a few basic disciplines that seem to work particularly well in conquering this difficulty. It's no surprise, therefore, that these same disciplines can have a similar effect on your personal goal of cultivating a deep work habit.

To conclude, let's return one last time to my own example. As I noted earlier, when I first embraced 4DX I adopted the goal of publishing five peer-reviewed papers in the 2013–2014 academic year. This was an ambitious goal given that I had published only four papers the previous year (a feat I was proud of). Throughout this 4DX experiment, the clarity of this goal, coupled with the simple but unavoidable feedback of my lead measure scoreboard, pushed me to a level of depth I hadn't before achieved. In retrospect, it was not so much the intensity of my deep work periods that increased, but instead their regularity. Whereas I used to cluster my deep thinking near paper submission deadlines, the 4DX habit kept my mind concentrated throughout the full year. It ended up, I must admit, an exhausting year (especially given that I was writing this book at the same time). But it also turned out to produce a convincing endorsement for the 4DX framework: By the summer of 2014, I had *nine* full papers accepted for publication, more than doubling what I had managed to accomplish in any preceding year.

Be Lazy

In a 2012 article written for a *New York Times* blog, the essayist and cartoonist Tim Kreider provided a memorable self-description: "I am not busy. I am the laziest ambitious person I know." Kreider's distaste for frenetic work, however, was put to the test in the months leading up to the writing of his post. Here's his description of the period: "I've insidiously started, because of professional obligations, to become busy... every morning my in-box was full of e-mails asking me to do things I did not want to do or presenting me with problems that I now had to solve."

His solution? He fled to what he calls an "undisclosed location": a place with no TV and no Internet (going online requires a bike ride to the local library), and where he could remain nonresponsive to the pinprick onslaught of small obligations that seem harmless in isolation but aggregate to serious injury to his deep work habit. "I've remembered about buttercups, stink bugs and the stars," Kreider says about his retreat from activity. "I read. And I'm finally getting some real writing done for the first time in months."

It's important for our purposes to recognize that Kreider is no Thoreau. He didn't retreat from the world of busyness to underscore a complicated social critique. His move to an undisclosed location was instead motivated by a surprising but practical insight: *It made him better at his job.* Here's Kreider's explanation:

> *Idleness is not just a vacation, an indulgence or a vice; it is as indispensable to the brain as vitamin D is to the body, and deprived of it we suffer a mental affliction as disfiguring as rickets... it is, paradoxically, necessary to getting any work done.*

When Kreider talks of getting work done, of course, he's not referencing shallow tasks. For the most part, the more time you can spend immersed in shallow work the more of it that gets accomplished. As a writer and artist, however, Kreider is instead concerned with deep work—the serious efforts that produce things the world values. These efforts, he's convinced, need the support of a mind regularly released to leisure.

This strategy argues that you should follow Kreider's lead by injecting regular and substantial freedom from professional concerns into your day, providing you with the idleness paradoxically required to get (deep) work done. There are many ways to accomplish this goal. You could, for example, use Kreider's approach of retreating from the world of shallow tasks altogether by hiding out in an "undisclosed location," but this isn't practical for most people. Instead, I want to suggest a more applicable but still quite powerful heuristic: At the end of the workday, shut down your consideration of work issues until the next morning—no after-dinner e-mail check, no mental replays of conversations, and no scheming about how you'll handle an upcoming challenge; shut down work thinking completely. If you need more time, then extend your workday, but once you shut down, your mind must be left free to encounter Kreider's buttercups, stink bugs, and stars.

Before describing some tactics that support this strategy, I want to first explore *why* a shutdown will be profitable to your ability to produce valuable output. We have, of course, Tim Kreider's personal endorsement, but it's worth taking the time to also understand the science behind the value of downtime. A closer examination of this literature reveals the following three possible explanations for this value.

Reason #1: Downtime Aids Insights

Consider the following excerpt from a 2006 paper that appeared in the journal *Science*:

> *The scientific literature has emphasized the benefits of conscious deliberation in decision making for hundreds of years... The question addressed here is whether this view is justified. We hypothesize that it is not.*

Lurking in this bland statement is a bold claim. The authors of this study, led by the Dutch psychologist Ap Dijksterhuis, set out to prove that some decisions are better left to your unconscious mind to untangle. In other words, to actively try to work through these decisions will lead to a *worse* outcome than loading up the relevant information and then moving on to something else while letting the subconscious layers of your mind mull things over.

Dijksterhuis's team isolated this effect by giving subjects the information needed for a complex decision regarding a car purchase. Half the subjects were told to think through the information and then make the best decision. The other half were distracted by easy puzzles after they read the information, and were then put on the spot to make a decision without having had time to consciously deliberate. The distracted group ended up performing better.

Observations from experiments such as this one led Dijksterhuis and his collaborators to introduce unconscious thought theory (UTT)—an attempt to understand the different roles conscious and unconscious deliberation play in decision making. At a high level, this theory proposes that for decisions that require the application of strict rules, the conscious mind must be involved. For example, if you need to do a math calculation, only your conscious mind is able to follow the precise arithmetic rules needed for correctness. On the other hand, for decisions that involve large amounts of information and multiple vague, and perhaps even conflicting, constraints, your unconscious mind is well suited to tackle the issue. UTT hypothesizes that this is due to the fact that these regions of your brain have more neuronal bandwidth available, allowing them to move around more information and sift through more potential solutions than your conscious centers of thinking. Your conscious mind, according to this theory, is like a home computer on which you can run carefully written programs that return correct answers to limited problems, whereas your unconscious mind is like Google's vast data centers, in which statistical algorithms sift through terabytes of unstructured information, teasing out surprising useful solutions to difficult questions.

The implication of this line of research is that providing your conscious brain time to rest enables your unconscious mind to take a shift sorting through your most complex professional challenges. A shutdown habit, therefore, is not necessarily reducing the amount of time you're engaged in productive work, but is instead diversifying the type of work you deploy.

Reason #2: Downtime Helps Recharge the Energy Needed to Work Deeply

A frequently cited 2008 paper appearing in the journal *Psychological Science* describes a simple experiment. Subjects were split into two groups. One group was asked to take a walk on a wooded path in an arboretum near the Ann Arbor, Michigan, campus where the study was conducted. The other group was sent on a walk through the bustling center of the city. Both groups were then given a concentration-sapping task called backward digit-span. The core finding of the study is that the nature group performed up to 20 percent better on the task. The nature advantage still held the next week when the researchers brought back the same subjects and switched the locations: It wasn't the people who determined performance, but whether or not they got a chance to prepare by walking through the woods.

This study, it turns out, is one of many that validate attention restoration theory (ART), which claims that spending time in nature can improve your ability to concentrate. This theory, which was first proposed in the 1980s by the University of Michigan psychologists Rachel Kaplan and Stephen Kaplan (the latter of which co-authored the 2008 study discussed here, along with Marc Berman and John Jonides), is based on the concept of attention fatigue. To concentrate requires what ART calls *directed attention*. This resource is finite: If you exhaust it, you'll struggle to concentrate. (For our purposes, we can think of this resource as the same thing as Baumeister's limited willpower reserves we discussed in the introduction to this rule.*) The 2008 study argues that walking on busy city streets requires you to use directed attention, as you must navigate complicated tasks like figuring out when to cross a street to not get run over, or when to maneuver around the slow group of tourists blocking the sidewalk. After just fifty minutes of this focused navigation, the subject's store of directed attention was low.

Walking through nature, by contrast, exposes you to what lead author Marc Berman calls "inherently fascinating stimuli," using sunsets as an example. These stimuli "invoke

---

* There is some debate in the literature as to whether these are the exact same quantity. For our purposes, however, this doesn't matter. The key observation is that there is a limited resource, necessary to attention, that must be conserved.

attention modestly, allowing focused-attention mechanisms a chance to replenish." Put another way, when walking through nature, you're freed from having to direct your attention, as there are few challenges to navigate (like crowded street crossings), and experience enough interesting stimuli to keep your mind sufficiently occupied to avoid the need to actively aim your attention. This state allows your directed attention resources time to replenish. After fifty minutes of such replenishment, the subjects enjoyed a boost in their concentration.

(You might, of course, argue that perhaps being outside watching a sunset puts people in a good mood, and being in a good mood is what really helps performance on these tasks. But in a sadistic twist, the researchers debunked that hypothesis by repeating the experiment in the harsh Ann Arbor winter. Walking outside in brutal cold conditions didn't put the subjects in a good mood, but they still ended up doing better on concentration tasks.)

What's important to our purpose is observing that the implications of ART expand beyond the benefits of nature. The core mechanism of this theory is the idea that you can restore your ability to direct your attention if you give this activity a rest. Walking in nature provides such a mental respite, but so, too, can any number of relaxing activities so long as they provide similar "inherently fascinating stimuli" and freedom from directed concentration. Having a casual conversation with a friend, listening to music while making dinner, playing a game with your kids, going for a run— the types of activities that will fill your time in the evening if you enforce a work shutdown—play the same attention-restoring role as walking in nature.

On the other hand, if you keep interrupting your evening to check and respond to e-mail, or put aside a few hours after dinner to catch up on an approaching deadline, you're robbing your directed attention centers of the uninterrupted rest they need for restoration. Even if these work dashes consume only a small amount of time, they prevent you from reaching the levels of deeper relaxation in which attention restoration can occur. Only the confidence that you're done with work until the next day can convince your brain to downshift to the level where it can begin to recharge for the next day to follow. Put another way, trying to squeeze a little more work out of your evenings might reduce your effectiveness the next day enough that you end up getting *less* done than if you had instead respected a shutdown.

Reason #3: *The Work That Evening Downtime Replaces Is Usually Not That Important*

The final argument for maintaining a clear endpoint to your workday requires us to return briefly to Anders Ericsson, the inventor of deliberate practice theory. As you might recall from Part 1, deliberate practice is the systematic stretching of your ability for a given skill. It is the activity required to get better at something. Deep work and deliberate practice, as I've argued, overlap substantially. For our purposes here we can use deliberate practice as a general-purpose stand-in for cognitively demanding efforts.

In Ericsson's seminal 1993 paper on the topic, titled

"The Role of Deliberate Practice in the Acquisition of Expert Performance," he dedicates a section to reviewing what the research literature reveals about an individual's capacity for cognitively demanding work. Ericsson notes that for a novice, somewhere around an hour a day of intense concentration seems to be a limit, while for experts this number can expand to as many as four hours—but rarely more.

One of the studies cited, for example, catalogs the practice habits of a group of elite violin players training at Berlin's Universität der Künste. This study found the elite players average around three and a half hours per day in a state of deliberate practice, usually separated into two distinct periods. The less accomplished players spent less time in a state of depth.

The implication of these results is that your capacity for deep work in a given day is limited. If you're careful about your schedule (using, for example, the type of productivity strategies described in Rule #4), you should hit your daily deep work capacity during your workday. It follows, therefore, that by evening, you're beyond the point where you can continue to effectively work deeply. Any work you do fit into the night, therefore, won't be the type of high-value activities that really advance your career; your efforts will instead likely be confined to low-value shallow tasks (executed at a slow, low-energy pace). By deferring evening work, in other words, you're not missing out on much of importance.

The three reasons just described support the general strategy of maintaining a strict endpoint to your workday. Let's conclude by filling in some details concerning implementation.

To succeed with this strategy, you must first accept the commitment that once your workday shuts down, you cannot allow even the smallest incursion of professional concerns into your field of attention. This includes, crucially, checking e-mail, as well as browsing work-related websites. In both cases, even a brief intrusion of work can generate a self-reinforcing stream of distraction that impedes the shutdown advantages described earlier for a long time to follow (most people are familiar, for example, with the experience of glancing at an alarming e-mail on a Saturday morning and then having its implications haunt your thoughts for the rest of the weekend).

Another key commitment for succeeding with this strategy is to support your commitment to shutting down with a strict *shutdown ritual* that you use at the end of the workday to maximize the probability that you succeed. In more detail, this ritual should ensure that every incomplete task, goal, or project has been reviewed and that for each you have confirmed that either (1) you have a plan you trust for its completion, or (2) it's captured in a place where it will be revisited when the time is right. The process should be an algorithm: a series of steps you always conduct, one after another. When you're done, have a set phrase you say that indicates completion (to end my own ritual, I say, "Shutdown complete"). This final step sounds cheesy, but it provides a simple cue to your mind that it's safe to release work-related thoughts for the rest of the day.

To make this suggestion more concrete, let me walk through the steps of my own shutdown ritual (which I first

developed around the time I was writing my doctoral dissertation, and have deployed, in one form or another, ever since).
The first thing I do is take a final look at my e-mail inbox
to ensure that there's nothing requiring an urgent response
before the day ends. The next thing I do is transfer any new
tasks that are on my mind or were scribbled down earlier
in the day into my official task lists. (I use Google Docs
for storing my task lists, as I like the ability to access them
from any computer—but the technology here isn't really
relevant.) Once I have these task lists open, I quickly skim
every task in every list, and then look at the next few days on
my calendar. These two actions ensure that there's nothing
urgent I'm forgetting or any important deadlines or appointments sneaking up on me. I have, at this point, reviewed
everything that's on my professional plate. To end the ritual,
I use this information to make a rough plan for the next day.
Once the plan is created, I say, "Shutdown complete," and
my work thoughts are done for the day.

The concept of a shutdown ritual might at first seem
extreme, but there's a good reason for it: the Zeigarnik effect.
This effect, which is named for the experimental work of
the early-twentieth-century psychologist Bluma Zeigarnik,
describes the ability of incomplete tasks to dominate our
attention. It tells us that if you simply stop whatever you are
doing at five p.m. and declare, "I'm done with work until
tomorrow," you'll likely struggle to keep your mind clear of
professional issues, as the many obligations left unresolved
in your mind will, as in Bluma Zeigarnik's experiments,

keep battling for your attention throughout the evening (a battle that they'll often win).

At first, this challenge might seem unresolvable. As any busy knowledge worker can attest, there are *always* tasks left incomplete. The idea that you can ever reach a point where all your obligations are handled is a fantasy. Fortunately, we don't need to *complete* a task to get it off our minds. Riding to our rescue in this matter is our friend from earlier in the rule, the psychologist Roy Baumeister, who wrote a paper with E.J. Masicampo playfully titled "Consider It Done!" In this study, the two researchers began by replicating the Zeigarnik effect in their subjects (in this case, the researchers assigned a task and then cruelly engineered interruptions), but then found that they could significantly reduce the effect's impact by asking the subjects, soon after the interruption, to make a plan for how they would *later* complete the incomplete task. To quote the paper: "Committing to a specific plan for a goal may therefore not only facilitate attainment of the goal but may also free cognitive resources for other pursuits."

The shutdown ritual described earlier leverages this tactic to battle the Zeigarnik effect. While it doesn't force you to explicitly identify a plan for every single task in your task list (a burdensome requirement), it does force you to capture every task in a common list, and then review these tasks before making a plan for the next day. This ritual ensures that no task will be forgotten: Each will be reviewed daily and tackled when the time is appropriate. Your mind, in other words, is released from its duty to keep track of these obligations at every moment—your shutdown ritual has taken over that responsibility.

Shutdown rituals can become annoying, as they add an extra ten to fifteen minutes to the end of your workday (and sometimes even more), but they're necessary for reaping the rewards of systematic idleness summarized previously. From my experience, it should take a week or two before the shutdown habit sticks—that is, until your mind trusts your ritual enough to actually begin to release work-related thoughts in the evening. But once it does stick, the ritual will become a permanent fixture in your life—to the point that skipping the routine will fill you with a sense of unease.

Decades of work from multiple different subfields within psychology all point toward the conclusion that regularly resting your brain improves the quality of your deep work. When you work, work hard. When you're done, be done. Your average e-mail response time might suffer some, but you'll more than make up for this with the sheer volume of truly important work produced during the day by your refreshed ability to dive deeper than your exhausted peers.

Embrace Boredom

To better understand how one masters the art of deep work, I suggest visiting the Knesses Yisroel Synagogue in Spring Valley, New York, at six a.m. on a weekday morning. If you do, you'll likely find at least twenty cars in the parking lot. Inside, you'll encounter a couple dozen members of the congregation working over texts—some might be reading silently, mouthing the words of an ancient language, while others are paired together debating. At one end of the room a rabbi will be leading a larger group in a discussion. This early morning gathering in Spring Valley represents just a small fraction of the hundreds of thousands of orthodox Jews who will wake up early that morning, as they do every weekday morning, to practice a central tenet of their faith: to spend time every day studying the complex written traditions of Rabbinic Judaism.

I was introduced to this world by Adam Marlin, a member of the Knesses Yisroel congregation and one of the regulars at its morning study group. As Marlin explained to me, his goal with this practice is to decipher one Talmud page each day (though he sometimes fails to make it even this far), often working with a *chevruta* (study partner) to push his understanding closer to his cognitive limit.

What interests me about Marlin is not his knowledge of ancient texts, but instead the type of effort required to gain this knowledge. When I interviewed him, he emphasized the mental intensity of his morning ritual. "It's an extreme and serious discipline, consisting mostly of the 'deep work' stuff [you write about]," he explained. "I run a growing business, but this is often the hardest brain strain I do." This strain is not unique to Marlin but is instead ingrained in the practice—as his rabbi once explained to him: "You cannot consider yourself as fulfilling this daily obligation unless you have stretched to the reaches of your mental capacity."

Unlike many orthodox Jews, Marlin came late to his faith, not starting his rigorous Talmud training until his twenties. This bit of trivia proves useful to our purposes because it allows Marlin a clear before-and-after comparison concerning the impact of these mental calisthenics—and the result surprised him. Though Marlin was exceptionally well educated when he began the practice—he holds *three different* Ivy League degrees—he soon met fellow adherents who had only ever attended small religious schools but could still "dance intellectual circles" around him. "A number of these people are highly successful [professionally]," he explained to me, "but it wasn't some fancy school that pushed their intellect higher; it became clear it was instead their daily study that started as early as the fifth grade."

After a while, Marlin began to notice positive changes in his own ability to think deeply. "I've recently been making more highly creative insights in my business life," he told me. "I'm convinced it's related to this daily mental practice. This consistent strain has built my mental muscle over years and years. This was not the goal when I started, but it is the effect."

———

Adam Marlin's experience underscores an important reality about deep work: The ability to concentrate intensely is a skill that must be trained. This idea might sound obvious once it's pointed out, but it represents a departure from how most people understand such matters. In my experience, it's common to treat undistracted concentration as a *habit* like flossing—something that you know how to do and know is good for you, but that you've been neglecting due to a lack of motivation. This mind-set is appealing because it implies you can transform your working life from distracted to focused overnight if you can simply muster enough motivation. But this understanding ignores the difficulty of focus and the hours of practice necessary to strengthen your "mental muscle." The creative insights that Adam Marlin now experiences in his professional life, in other words, have little to do with a onetime decision to think deeper, and much to do with a commitment to training this ability early every morning.

There is, however, an important corollary to this idea: Efforts to deepen your focus will struggle if you don't simultaneously wean your mind from a dependence on distraction. Much in the same way that athletes must take care of their bodies outside of their training sessions, you'll struggle to achieve the deepest levels of concentration if you spend the rest of your time fleeing the slightest hint of boredom.

We can find evidence for this claim in the research of Clifford Nass, the late Stanford communications professor who was well known for his study of behavior in the digital age. Among other insights, Nass's research revealed that constant attention switching online has a lasting negative effect on your brain. Here's Nass summarizing these findings in a 2010 interview with NPR's Ira Flatow:

> *So we have scales that allow us to divide up people into people who multitask all the time and people who rarely do, and the differences are remarkable. People who multitask all the time can't filter out irrelevancy. They can't manage a working memory. They're chronically distracted. They initiate much larger parts of their brain that are irrelevant to the task at hand... they're pretty much mental wrecks.*

At this point Flatow asks Nass whether the chronically distracted recognize this rewiring of their brain:

> *The people we talk with continually said, "look, when I really have to concentrate, I turn off everything and I am laser-focused."* And unfortunately, they've developed habits of mind that make it impossible for them to be laser-focused. *They're suckers for irrelevancy. They just can't keep on task.* [emphasis mine]

Once your brain has become accustomed to on-demand distraction, Nass discovered, it's hard to shake the addiction even when you *want* to concentrate. To put this more concretely: If every moment of potential boredom in your life—say, having to wait five minutes in line or sit alone in a restaurant until a friend arrives—is relieved with a quick glance at your smartphone, then your brain has likely been rewired to a point where, like the "mental wrecks" in Nass's research, it's not ready for deep work—even if you regularly schedule time to practice this concentration.

Rule #1 taught you how to integrate deep work into your schedule and support it with routines and rituals designed to help you consistently reach the current limit of your concentration ability. Rule #2 will help you significantly improve this limit. The strategies that follow are motivated by the key idea that getting the most out of your deep work habit requires training, and as clarified previously, this training must address two goals: improving your ability to concentrate intensely *and* overcoming your desire for distraction. These strategies cover a variety of approaches, from quarantining distraction to mastering a special form of meditation, that combine to provide a practical road map for your journey from a mind wrecked by constant distraction and unfamiliar with concentration, to an instrument that truly does deliver laser-like focus.

Don't Take Breaks from Distraction. Instead Take Breaks from Focus.

Many assume that they can switch between a state of distraction and one of concentration as needed, but as I just argued, this assumption is optimistic: Once you're wired for distraction, you crave it. Motivated by this reality, this strategy is designed to help you rewire your brain to a configuration better suited to staying on task.

Before diving into the details, let's start by considering a popular suggestion for distraction addiction that doesn't quite solve our problem: the Internet Sabbath (sometimes called a digital detox). In its basic form, this ritual asks you to put aside regular time—typically, one day a week—where you refrain from network technology. In the same way that the Sabbath in the Hebrew Bible induces a period of quiet and reflection well suited to appreciate God and his works, the Internet Sabbath is meant to remind you of what you miss when you are glued to a screen.

It's unclear who first introduced the Internet Sabbath concept, but credit for popularizing the idea often goes to the journalist William Powers, who promoted the practice in his 2010 reflection on technology and human happiness, *Hamlet's BlackBerry*. As Powers later summarizes in an interview: "Do what Thoreau did, which is learn to have a little disconnectedness within the connected world—don't run away."

A lot of advice for the problem of distraction follows this general template of finding occasional time to get away from the clatter. Some put aside one or two months a year to escape these tethers, others follow Powers's one-day-a-week advice, while others put aside an hour or two every day for the same purpose. All forms of this advice provide some benefit, but once we see the distraction problem in terms of brain wiring, it becomes clear that an Internet Sabbath cannot by itself cure a distracted brain. If you eat healthy just one day a week, you're unlikely to lose weight, as the majority of your time is still spent gorging. Similarly, if you spend just one day a week resisting distraction, you're unlikely to diminish your brain's craving for these stimuli, as most of your time is still spent giving in to it.

I propose an alternative to the Internet Sabbath. Instead of scheduling the occasional break *from distraction* so you can focus, you should instead schedule the occasional break *from focus* to give in to distraction. To make this suggestion more concrete, let's make the simplifying assumption that Internet use is synonymous with seeking distracting stimuli. (You can, of course, use the Internet in a way that's focused and deep, but for a distraction addict, this is a difficult task.) Similarly, let's consider working in the absence of the Internet to be synonymous with more focused work. (You can, of course, find ways to be distracted without a network connection, but these tend to be easier to resist.)

With these rough categorizations established, the strategy works as follows: Schedule in advance when you'll use the Internet, and then avoid it altogether outside these times. I suggest that you keep a notepad near your computer at work. On this pad, record the *next* time you're allowed to use the Internet. Until you arrive at that time, absolutely no network connectivity is allowed—no matter how tempting.

The idea motivating this strategy is that the use of a distracting service does not, by itself, reduce your brain's ability to focus. It's instead the constant *switching* from low-stimuli/high-value activities to high-stimuli/low-value activities, at the slightest hint of boredom or cognitive challenge, that teaches your mind to never tolerate an absence of novelty. This constant switching can be understood analogously as weakening the mental muscles responsible for organizing the many sources vying for your attention. By segregating Internet use (and therefore segregating distractions) you're minimizing the number of times you give in to distraction, and by doing so you let these attention-selecting muscles strengthen.

For example, if you've scheduled your next Internet block thirty minutes from the current moment, and you're beginning to feel bored and crave distraction, the next thirty minutes of resistance become a session of concentration calisthenics. A full day of scheduled distraction therefore becomes a full day of similar mental training.

While the basic idea behind this strategy is straightforward, putting it into practice can be tricky. To help you succeed, here are three important points to consider.

Point #1: *This strategy works even if your job requires lots of Internet use and/or prompt e-mail replies.*

If you're required to spend hours every day online or answer e-mails quickly, that's fine: This simply means that your *Internet blocks* will be more numerous than those of someone whose job requires less connectivity. The total number or duration of your Internet blocks doesn't matter nearly as much as making sure that the integrity of your *offline blocks* remains intact.

Imagine, for example, that over a two-hour period between meetings, you must schedule an e-mail check every fifteen minutes. Further imagine that these checks require, on average, five minutes. It's sufficient, therefore, to schedule an Internet block every fifteen minutes through this two-hour stretch, with the rest of the time dedicated to offline blocks. In this example, you'll end up spending around ninety minutes out of this two-hour period in a state where you're offline and actively resisting distraction. This works out to be a large amount of concentration training that's achieved without requiring you to sacrifice too much connectivity.

Point #2: *Regardless of how you schedule your Internet blocks, you must keep the time outside these blocks absolutely free from Internet use.*

This objective is easy to state in principle but quickly becomes tricky in the messy reality of the standard workday. An inevitable issue you'll face when executing this strategy is realizing early on in an offline block that there's some crucial piece of information online that you need to retrieve to continue making progress on your current task. If your next Internet block doesn't start for a while, you might end up stuck. The temptation in this situation is to quickly give in, look up the information, then return to your offline block. *You must resist this temptation!* The Internet is seductive: You may think you're just retrieving a single key e-mail from your inbox, but you'll find it hard to not glance at the other "urgent" messages that have recently arrived. It doesn't take many of these exceptions before your mind begins to treat the barrier between Internet and offline blocks as permeable—diminishing the benefits of this strategy.

It's crucial in this situation, therefore, that you don't immediately abandon an offline block, even when stuck. If it's possible, switch to another offline activity for the remainder of the current block (or perhaps even fill in this time relaxing). If this is infeasible—perhaps you need to get the current offline activity done promptly—then the correct response is to *change* your schedule so that your next Internet block begins sooner. The key in making this change, however, is to not schedule the next Internet block to occur immediately. Instead, enforce at least a five-minute gap between the current moment and the next time you can go online. This gap is minor, so it won't excessively impede your progress, but from a behavioralist perspective, it's substantial because it separates the sensation of wanting to go online from the reward of actually doing so.

Point #3: Scheduling Internet use at home as well as at work can further improve your concentration training.

If you find yourself glued to a smartphone or laptop throughout your evenings and weekends, then it's likely that your behavior outside of work is undoing many of your attempts during the workday to rewire your brain (which makes little distinction between the two settings). In this case, I would suggest that you maintain the strategy of scheduling Internet use even after the workday is over.

To simplify matters, when scheduling Internet use after work, you can allow time-sensitive communication into your offline blocks (e.g., texting with a friend to agree on where you'll meet for dinner), as well as time-sensitive information retrieval (e.g., looking up the location of the restaurant on your phone). Outside of these pragmatic exceptions, however, when in an offline block, put your phone away, ignore texts, and refrain from Internet usage. As in the workplace variation of this strategy, if the Internet plays a large and important role in your evening entertainment, that's fine: Schedule lots of long Internet blocks. The key here isn't to avoid or even to reduce the total amount of time you spend engaging in distracting behavior, but is instead to give yourself plenty of opportunities throughout your evening to *resist* switching to these distractions at the slightest hint of boredom.

One place where this strategy becomes particularly difficult outside work is when you're forced to wait (for example, standing in line at a store). It's crucial in these situations that if you're in an offline block, you simply gird yourself for the temporary boredom, and fight through it with only the company of your thoughts. To simply wait and be bored has become a novel experience in modern life, but from the perspective of concentration training, it's incredibly valuable.

To summarize, to succeed with deep work you must rewire your brain to be comfortable resisting distracting stimuli. This doesn't mean that you have to eliminate distracting behaviors; it's sufficient that you instead eliminate the ability of such behaviors to hijack your attention. The simple strategy proposed here of scheduling Internet blocks goes a long way toward helping you regain this attention autonomy.

Work Like Teddy Roosevelt

If you attended Harvard College during the 1876–1877 school year, you would've likely noticed a wiry, mutton-chopped, brash, and impossibly energetic freshman named Theodore Roosevelt. If you then proceeded to befriend this young man, you would've soon noticed a paradox.

On the one hand, his attention might appear to be hopelessly scattered, spread over what one classmate called an "amazing array of interests"—a list that biographer Edmund Morris catalogs to contain boxing, wrestling, body building, dance lessons, poetry readings, and the continuation of a lifelong obsession with naturalism (Roosevelt's landlord on Winthrop Street was not pleased with her young tenant's tendency to dissect and stuff specimens in his rented room). This latter interest developed to the point that Roosevelt published his first book, *The Summer Birds of the Adirondacks*, in the summer after his freshman year. It was well received in the *Bulletin of the Nuttall Ornithological Club*— a publication, needless to say, which takes bird books quite seriously—and was good enough to lead Morris to assess Roosevelt, at this young age, to be "one of the most knowledgeable young naturalists in the United States."

To support this extracurricular exuberance Roosevelt had to severely restrict the time left available for what should have been his primary focus: his studies at Harvard. Morris

used Roosevelt's diary and letters from this period to estimate that the future president was spending no more than a
quarter of the typical day studying. One might expect therefore that Roosevelt's grades would crater. But they didn't. He
wasn't the top student in his class, but he certainly didn't
struggle either: In his freshman year he earned honor grades
in five out of his seven courses. The explanation for this
Roosevelt paradox turns out to be his unique approach to
tackling this schoolwork. Roosevelt would begin his scheduling by considering the eight hours from eight thirty a.m.
to four thirty p.m. He would then remove the time spent in
recitation and classes, his athletic training (which was once
a day), and lunch. The fragments that remained were then
considered time dedicated exclusively to studying. As noted,
these fragments didn't usually add up to a large number of
total hours, but he would get the most out of them by working *only* on schoolwork during these periods, and doing so
with a blistering *intensity*. "The amount of time he spent at
his desk was comparatively small," explained Morris, "but
his concentration was so intense, and his reading so rapid,
that he could afford more time off [from schoolwork] than
most."

This strategy asks you to inject the occasional dash of Rooseveltian intensity into your own workday. In particular, identify a deep task (that is, something that requires deep work
to complete) that's high on your priority list. Estimate how
long you'd normally put aside for an obligation of this type,
then give yourself a hard deadline that *drastically reduces*

this time. If possible, commit publicly to the deadline—for example, by telling the person expecting the finished project when they should expect it. If this isn't possible (or if it puts your job in jeopardy), then motivate yourself by setting a countdown timer on your phone and propping it up where you can't avoid seeing it as you work.

At this point, there should be only one possible way to get the deep task done in time: *working with great intensity*—no e-mail breaks, no daydreaming, no Facebook browsing, no repeated trips to the coffee machine. Like Roosevelt at Harvard, attack the task with every free neuron until it gives way under your unwavering barrage of concentration.

Try this experiment no more than once a week at first—giving your brain practice with intensity, but also giving it (and your stress levels) time to rest in between. Once you feel confident in your ability to trade concentration for completion time, increase the frequency of these Roosevelt dashes. Remember, however, to always keep your self-imposed deadlines right at the edge of feasibility. You should be able to consistently beat the buzzer (or at least be close), but to do so should require teeth-gritting concentration.

The main motivation for this strategy is straightforward. Deep work requires levels of concentration well beyond where most knowledge workers are comfortable. Roosevelt dashes leverage artificial deadlines to help you systematically increase the level you can regularly achieve—providing, in some sense, interval training for the attention centers of your brain. An additional benefit is that these dashes are incompatible with distraction (there's no way you can give in to distraction and still make your deadlines). Therefore, every completed dash provides a session in which you're potentially bored, and really want to seek more novel stimuli—but you resist. As argued in the previous strategy, the more you practice resisting such urges, the easier such resistance becomes.

After a few months of deploying this strategy, your understanding of what it means to focus will likely be transformed as you reach levels of intensity stronger than anything you've experienced before. And if you're anything like a young Roosevelt, you can then repurpose the extra free time it generates toward the finer pleasures in life, like trying to impress the always-discerning members of the Nuttall Ornithological Club.

Meditate Productively

During the two years I spent as a postdoctoral associate at MIT, my wife and I lived in a small but charming apartment on Pinckney Street, in historic Beacon Hill. Though I lived in Boston and worked in Cambridge, the two locations were close—only a mile apart, sitting on opposite banks of the Charles River. Intent on staying fit, even during the long and dark New England winter, I decided to take advantage of this proximity by traveling between home and work, to the greatest extent possible, on foot.

My routine had me walk to campus in the morning, crossing the Longfellow Bridge in all weather (the city, it turns out to my dismay, is often slow to shovel the pedestrian path after snowstorms). Around lunch, I would change into running gear and run back home on a longer path that followed the banks of the Charles, crossing at the Massachusetts Avenue Bridge. After a quick lunch and shower at home, I would typically take the subway across the river on the way back to campus (saving, perhaps, a third of a mile on the trek), and then walk home when the workday was done. In other words, I spent *a lot* of time on my feet during this period. It was this reality that led me to develop the practice that I'll now suggest you adopt in your own deep work training: *productive meditation*.

The goal of productive meditation is to take a period in which you're occupied physically but not mentally—walking, jogging, driving, showering—and focus your attention on a single well-defined professional problem. Depending on your profession, this problem might be outlining an article, writing a talk, making progress on a proof, or attempting to sharpen a business strategy. As in mindfulness meditation, you must continue to bring your attention back to the problem at hand when it wanders or stalls.

I used to practice productive meditation in at least one of my daily cross-river treks while living in Boston, and as I improved, so did my results. I ended up, for example, working out the chapter outlines for a significant portion of my last book while on foot, and made progress on many knotty technical problems in my academic research.

I suggest that you adopt a productive meditation practice in your own life. You don't necessarily need a serious session every day, but your goal should be to participate in at least two or three such sessions in a typical week. Fortunately, finding time for this strategy is easy, as it takes advantage of periods that would otherwise be wasted (such as walking the dog or commuting to work), and if done right, can actually increase your professional productivity instead of taking time away from your work. In fact, you might even consider scheduling a walk during your workday specifically for the purpose of applying productive meditation to your most pressing problem at the moment.

I'm not, however, suggesting this practice for its productivity benefits (though they're nice). I'm instead interested in its ability to rapidly improve your ability to think deeply. In my experience, productive meditation builds on both of the key ideas introduced at the beginning of this rule. By forcing you to resist distraction and return your attention repeatedly to a well-defined problem, it helps strengthen your distraction-resisting muscles, and by forcing you to push your focus deeper and deeper on a single problem, it sharpens your concentration.

To succeed with productive meditation, it's important to recognize that, like any form of meditation, it requires practice to do well. When I first attempted this strategy, back in the early weeks of my postdoc, I found myself hopelessly distracted—ending long stretches of "thinking" with little new to show for my efforts. It took me a dozen or so sessions before I began to experience real results. You should expect something similar, so patience will be necessary. To help accelerate this ramp-up process, however, I have two specific suggestions to offer.

Suggestion #1: Be Wary of Distractions and Looping

As a novice, when you begin a productive meditation session, your mind's first act of rebellion will be to offer unrelated but seemingly more interesting thoughts. My mind, for example, was often successful at derailing my attention by beginning to compose an e-mail that I knew I needed to write. Objectively speaking, this train of thought sounds exceedingly dull, but in the moment it can become impossibly tantalizing. When you notice your attention slipping away from the problem at hand, gently remind yourself that you can return to that thought later, then redirect your attention back.

Distraction of this type, in many ways, is the obvious enemy to defeat in developing a productive meditation habit. A subtler, but equally effective adversary, is looping. When faced with a hard problem, your mind, as it was evolved to do, will attempt to avoid excess expenditure of energy when possible. One way it might attempt to sidestep this expenditure is by avoiding diving deeper into the problem by instead looping over and over again on what you already know about it. For example, when working on a proof, my mind has a tendency to rehash simple preliminary results, again and again, to avoid the harder work of building on these results toward the needed solution. You must be on your guard for looping, as it can quickly subvert an entire productive meditation session. When you notice it, remark to yourself that you seem to be in a loop, then redirect your attention toward the next step.

Suggestion #2: *Structure Your Deep Thinking*

"Thinking deeply" about a problem seems like a self-evident activity, but in reality it's not. When faced with a distraction-free mental landscape, a hard problem, and time to think, the next steps can become surprisingly non-obvious. In my experience, it helps to have some structure for this deep thinking process. I suggest starting with a careful review of the relevant *variables* for solving the problem and then storing these values in your working memory. For example, if you're working on the outline for a book chapter, the relevant variables might be the main points you want to make in the chapter. If you're instead trying to solve a mathematics proof, these variables might be actual variables, or assumptions, or lemmas. Once the relevant variables are identified, define the specific *next-step question* you need to answer using these variables. In the book chapter example, this next-step question might be, "How am I going to effectively open this chapter?," and for a proof it might be, "What can go wrong if I don't assume this property holds?" With the relevant variables stored and the next-step question identified, you now have a specific target for your attention.

Assuming you're able to solve your next-step question, the final step of this structured approach to deep thinking is to *consolidate* your gains by reviewing clearly the answer you identified. At this point, you can push yourself to the next level of depth by starting the process over. This cycle of reviewing and storing variables, identifying and tackling the next-step question, then consolidating your gains is like an intense workout routine for your concentration ability. It will help you get more out of your productive meditation sessions and accelerate the pace at which you improve your ability to go deep.

Memorize a Deck of Cards

Given just five minutes, Daniel Kilov can memorize any of the following: a shuffled deck of cards, a string of one hundred random digits, or 115 abstract shapes (this last feat establishing an Australian national record). It shouldn't be surprising, therefore, that Kilov recently won back-to-back silver medals in the Australian memory championships. What *is* perhaps surprising, given Kilov's history, is that he ended up a mental athlete at all.

"I wasn't born with an exceptional memory," Kilov told me. Indeed, during high school he considered himself forgetful and disorganized. He also struggled academically and was eventually diagnosed with attention deficit disorder. It was after a chance encounter with Tansel Ali, one of the country's most successful and visible memory champions, that Kilov began to seriously train his memory. By the time he earned his college degree he had won his first national competition medal.

This transformation into a world-class mental athlete was rapid, but not unprecedented. In 2006, the American science writer Joshua Foer won the USA Memory Championship after only a year of (intense) training—a journey he chronicled in his 2011 bestseller, *Moonwalking with Einstein*. But what's important to us about Kilov's story is what happened to his *academic* performance during this period of intensive memory development. While training his brain, he went from a struggling student with attention deficit disorder to graduating from a demanding Australian university with first-class honors. He was soon accepted into the PhD program at one of the country's top universities, where he currently studies under a renowned philosopher.

One explanation for this transformation comes from research led by Henry Roediger, who runs the Memory Lab at the University of Washington in Saint Louis. In 2014, Roediger and his collaborators sent a team, equipped with a battery of cognitive tests, to the Extreme Memory Tournament held in San Diego. They wanted to understand what differentiated these elite memorizers from the population at large. "We found that one of the biggest differences between memory athletes and the rest of us is in a cognitive ability that's not a direct measure of memory at all *but of attention*," explained Roediger in a *New York Times* blog post (emphasis mine). The ability in question is called "attentional control," and it measures the subjects' ability to maintain their focus on essential information.

A side effect of memory training, in other words, is an improvement in your general ability to concentrate. This ability can then be fruitfully applied to any task demanding deep work. Daniel Kilov, we can therefore conjecture, didn't become a star student because of his award-winning memory; it was instead his quest to improve this memory that (incidentally) gave him the deep work edge needed to thrive academically.

The strategy described here asks you to replicate a key piece of Kilov's training, and therefore gain some of the same improvements to your concentration. In particular, it asks you to learn a standard but quite impressive skill in the repertoire of most mental athletes: the ability to memorize a shuffled deck of cards.

———

The technique for card memorization I'll teach you comes from someone who knows quite a bit about this particular challenge: Ron White, a former USA Memory Champion and world record holder in card memorization.* The first thing White emphasizes is that professional memory athletes *never* attempt rote memorization, that is, where you simply look at information again and again, repeating it in your head. This approach to retention, though popular among burned-out students, misunderstands how our brains work. We're not wired to quickly internalize abstract information. We are, however, really good at remembering scenes. Think back to a recent memorable event in your life: perhaps attending the opening session of a conference or meeting a friend you haven't seen in a while for a drink. Try to picture

* The specific article by White from which I draw the steps presented here can be found online: Ron White, "How to Memorize a Deck of Cards with Superhuman Speed," guest post, *The Art of Manliness*, June 1, 2012, http://www.artofmanliness.com/2012/06/01/how-to-memorize -a-deck-of-cards/.

the scene as clearly as possible. Most people in this scenario can conjure a surprisingly vivid recollection of the event—even though you made no special effort to remember it at the time. If you systematically counted the unique details in this memory, the total number of items would likely be surprisingly numerous. Your mind, in other words, can quickly retain lots of detailed information—if it's stored in the right way. Ron White's card memorization technique builds on this insight.

To prepare for this high-volume memorization task, White recommends that you begin by cementing in your mind the mental image of walking through five rooms in your home. Perhaps you come in the door, walk through your front hallway, then turn into the downstairs bathroom, walk out the door and enter the guest bedroom, walk into the kitchen, and then head down the stairs into your basement. In each room, conjure a clear image of what you see.

Once you can easily recall this mental walkthrough of a well-known location, fix in your mind a collection of ten items in each of these rooms. White recommends that these items be large (and therefore more memorable), like a desk, not a pencil. Next, establish an order in which you look at each of these items in each room. For example, in the front hallway, you might look at the entry mat, then shoes on the floor by the mat, then the bench above the shoes, and so on. Combined this is only fifty items, so add two more items, perhaps in your backyard, to get to the full fifty-two items you'll later need when connecting these images to all the cards in a standard deck.

Practice this mental exercise of walking through the rooms, and looking at items in each room, in a set order. You should find that this type of memorization, because it's based on visual images of familiar places and things, will be much easier than the rote memorizing you might remember from your school days.

The second step in preparing to memorize a deck of cards is to associate a memorable person or thing with each of the fifty-two possible cards. To make this process easier, try to maintain some logical association between the card and the corresponding image. White provides the example of associating Donald Trump with the King of Diamonds, as diamonds signify wealth. Practice these associations until you can pull a card randomly from the deck and immediately recall the associated image. As before, the use of memorable visual images and associations will simplify the task of forming these connections.

The two steps mentioned previously are *advance* steps— things you do just once and can then leverage again and again in memorizing specific decks. Once these steps are done, you're ready for the main event: memorizing as quickly as possible the order of fifty-two cards in a freshly shuffled deck. The method here is straightforward. Begin your mental walk-through of your house. As you encounter each item, look at the next card from the shuffled deck, and imagine the corresponding memorable person or thing doing something memorable near that item. For example, if the first item and location is the mat in your front entry, and the first card is the King of Diamonds, you might picture Donald Trump wiping mud off of his expensive loafers on the entry mat in your front hallway.

Proceed carefully through the rooms, associating the proper mental images with objects in the proper order. After you complete a room, you might want to walk through it a few times in a row to lock in the imagery. Once you're done, you're ready to hand the deck to a friend and amaze him by rattling off the cards in order without peeking. To do so, of course, simply requires that you perform the mental walk-through one more time, connecting each memorable person or thing to its corresponding card as you turn your attention to it.

―――――――

If you practice this technique, you'll discover, like many mental athletes who came before you, that you can eventually internalize a whole deck in just minutes. More important than your ability to impress friends, of course, is the training such activities provide your mind. Proceeding through the steps described earlier requires that you focus your attention, again and again, on a clear target. Like a muscle respond-ing to weights, this will strengthen your general ability to concentrate—allowing you to go deeper with more ease.

It's worth emphasizing, however, the obvious point that there's nothing special about card memorization. Any struc-tured thought process that requires unwavering attention can have a similar effect—be it studying the Talmud, like Adam Marlin from Rule #2's introduction, or practicing productive meditation, or trying to learn the guitar part of a song by ear (a past favorite of mine). If card memorization seems weird to you, in other words, then choose a replacement that makes similar cognitive requirements. The key to this strategy is not the specifics, but instead the motivating idea that your ability to concentrate is only as strong as your commitment to train it.

Rule #3

Quit Social Media

In 2013, author and digital media consultant Baratunde Thurston launched an experiment. He decided to disconnect from his online life for twenty-five days: no Facebook, no Twitter, no Foursquare (a service that awarded him "Mayor of the Year" in 2011), not even e-mail. He needed the break. Thurston, who is described by friends as "the most connected man in the world," had by his own count participated in more than fifty-nine thousand Gmail conversations and posted fifteen hundred times on his Facebook wall in the year leading up to his experiment. "I was burnt out. Fried. Done. Toast," he explained.

We know about Thurston's experiment because he wrote about it in a cover article for *Fast Company* magazine, ironically titled "#UnPlug." As Thurston reveals in the article, it didn't take long to adjust to a disconnected life. "By the end of that first week, the quiet rhythm of my days seemed far less strange," he said. "I was less stressed about not knowing new things; I felt that I still existed despite not having shared documentary evidence of said existence on the Internet." Thurston struck up conversations with strangers. He enjoyed food without Instagramming the experience. He bought a bike ("turns out it's easier to ride the thing when you're not trying to simultaneously check your Twitter"). "The end came too soon," Thurston lamented. But he had start-ups to run and books to market, so after the twenty-five days passed, he reluctantly reactivated his online presence.

Baratunde Thurston's experiment neatly summarizes two important points about our culture's current relationship with social networks like Facebook, Twitter, and Instagram, and infotainment sites like Business Insider and BuzzFeed—two categories of online distraction that I will collectively call "network tools" in the pages ahead. The first point is that we increasingly recognize that these tools fragment our time and reduce our ability to concentrate. This reality no longer generates much debate; we all feel it. This is a real problem for many different people, but the problem is especially dire if you're attempting to improve your ability to work deeply. In the preceding rule, for example, I described several strategies to help you sharpen your focus. These efforts will become significantly more difficult if you simultaneously behave like a pre-experiment Baratunde Thurston, allowing your life outside such training to remain a distracted blur of apps and browser tabs. Willpower is limited, and therefore the more enticing tools you have pulling at your attention, the harder it'll be to maintain focus on something important. To master the art of deep work, therefore, you must take back control of your time and attention from the many diversions that attempt to steal them.

Before we begin fighting back against these distractions, however, we must better understand the battlefield. This brings me to the second important point summarized by Baratunde Thurston's story: the impotence with which knowledge workers currently discuss this problem of network tools and attention. Overwhelmed by these tools' demands on his time, Thurston felt that his only option was to (temporarily) quit the Internet altogether. This idea that a drastic *Internet sabbatical** is the only alternative to the distraction generated by social media and infotainment has increasingly pervaded our cultural conversation.

The problem with this binary response to this issue is that these two choices are much too crude to be useful. The notion that you would quit the Internet is, of course, an overstuffed straw man, infeasible for most (unless you're a journalist writing a piece about distraction). No one is meant to actually follow Baratunde Thurston's lead—and this reality provides justification for remaining with the only offered alternative: accepting our current distracted state as inevitable. For all the insight and clarity that Thurston gained during his Internet sabbatical, for example, it didn't take him long once the experiment ended to slide back into the fragmented state where he began. On the day when I

---

* Notice, the *Internet sabbatical* is not the same as the *Internet Sabbath* mentioned in Rule #2. The latter asks that you regularly take small breaks from the Internet (usually a single weekend day), while the former describes a substantial and long break from an online life, lasting many weeks—and sometimes more.

first starting writing this chapter, which fell only six months after Thurston's article originally appeared in *Fast Company*, the reformed connector had already sent a dozen Tweets in the few hours since he woke up.

This rule attempts to break us out of this rut by proposing a third option: accepting that these tools are not inherently evil, and that some of them might be quite vital to your success and happiness, *but at the same time* also accepting that the threshold for allowing a site regular access to your time and attention (not to mention personal data) should be much more stringent, and that most people should therefore be using many fewer such tools. I won't ask you, in other words, to quit the Internet altogether like Baratunde Thurston did for twenty-five days back in 2013. But I will ask you to reject the state of distracted hyperconnectedness that drove him to that drastic experiment in the first place. There is a middle ground, and if you're interested in developing a deep work habit, you must fight to get there.

Our first step toward finding this middle ground in network tool selection is to understand the current default decision process deployed by most Internet users. In the fall of 2013, I received insight into this process because of an article I wrote explaining why I never joined Facebook. Though the piece was meant to be explanatory and not accusatory, it nonetheless put many readers on the defensive, leading them to reply with justifications for *their* use of the service. Here are some examples of these justifications:

- "Entertainment was my initial draw to Facebook. I can see what my friends are up to and post funny photos, make quick comments."
- "[When] I first joined, [I didn't know why]...By mere curiosity I joined a forum of short fiction stories. [Once] there I improved my writing and made very good friends."
- "[I use] Facebook because a lot of people I knew in high school are on there."

Here's what strikes me about these responses (which are representative of the large amount of feedback I received on this topic): They're surprisingly minor. I don't doubt, for example, that the first commenter from this list finds some entertainment in using Facebook, but I would also assume that this person wasn't suffering some severe deficit of entertainment options before he or she signed up for the service. I would further wager that this user would succeed in staving off boredom even if the service were suddenly shut down. Facebook, at best, added one more (arguably quite mediocre) entertainment option to many that already existed.

Another commenter cited making friends in a writing forum. I don't doubt the existence of these friends, but we can assume that these friendships are lightweight—given that they're based on sending short messages back and forth over a computer network. There's nothing wrong with such lightweight friendships, but they're unlikely to be at the center of this user's social life. Something similar can be said about the commenter who reconnected with high school friends: This is a nice diversion, but hardly something central to his or her sense of social connection or happiness.

To be clear, I'm not trying to denigrate the benefits identified previously—there's nothing illusory or misguided about them. What I'm emphasizing, however, is that these benefits are minor and somewhat random. (By contrast, if you'd instead asked someone to justify the use of, say, the World Wide Web more generally, or e-mail, the arguments would become much more concrete and compelling.) To this observation, you might reply that *value is value*: If you can find some extra benefit in using a service like Facebook— even if it's small—then why not use it? I call this way of thinking the *any-benefit* mind-set, as it identifies any possible benefit as sufficient justification for using a network tool. In more detail:

The Any-Benefit Approach to Network Tool Selection: You're justified in using a network tool if you can identify *any* possible benefit to its use, or *anything* you might possibly miss out on if you don't use it.

The problem with this approach, of course, is that it ignores all the negatives that come along with the tools in question. These services are engineered to be addictive— robbing time and attention from activities that more directly support your professional and personal goals (such as deep work). Eventually, if you use these tools enough, you'll arrive at the state of burned-out, hyperdistracted connectivity that plagued Baratunde Thurston and millions of others like him. It's here that we encounter the true insidious nature of an any-benefit mind-set. The use of network tools can be harmful. If you don't attempt to weigh pros against cons, but instead use any glimpse of some potential benefit as justification for unrestrained use of a tool, then you're unwittingly crippling your ability to succeed in the world of knowledge work.

This conclusion, if considered objectively, shouldn't be surprising. In the context of network tools, we've become comfortable with the any-benefit mind-set, but if we instead zoom out and consider this mind-set in the broader context of skilled labor, it suddenly seems a bizarre and ahistorical approach to choosing tools. In other words, once you put aside the revolutionary rhetoric surrounding all things Internet—the sense, summarized in Part 1, that you're either fully committed to "the revolution" or a Luddite curmudgeon—you'll soon realize that network tools are not exceptional; they're tools, no different from a blacksmith's hammer or an artist's brush, used by skilled laborers to do their jobs better (and occasionally to enhance their leisure). Throughout history, skilled laborers have applied sophistication and skepticism to their encounters with new tools and their decisions about whether to adopt them. There's no reason why knowledge workers cannot do the same when it comes to the Internet—the fact that the skilled labor here now involves digital bits doesn't change this reality.

To help understand what this more careful tool curation might look like, it makes sense to start by talking to someone who makes a living working with (nondigital) tools and relies on a complex relationship with these tools to succeed. Fortunately for our purposes, I found just such an individual in a lanky English major turned successful sustainable farmer, named (almost too aptly), Forrest Pritchard.

Forrest Pritchard runs Smith Meadows, a family farm located an hour west of D.C.—one of many farms clustered in the valleys of the Blue Ridge Mountains. Soon after taking control of the land from his parents, as I learned, Pritchard moved the operation away from traditional monoculture crops and toward the then novel concept of grass-finished meat. The farm bypasses wholesaling—you cannot find Smith Meadows steaks in Whole Foods—to sell direct to consumers at the bustling farmers' markets in the Washington, D.C., metro area. By all accounts, the farm is thriving in an industry that rarely rewards small operations.

I first encountered Pritchard at our local farmers' market in Takoma Park, Maryland, where the Smith Meadows stand does good business. To see Pritchard, usually standing a foot taller than most of his suburbanite customers, wearing the obligatory faded flannel of the farmer, is to see a craftsman confident in his trade. I introduced myself to him because farming is a skill dependent on the careful management of tools, and I wanted to understand how a craftsman in a nondigital field approaches this crucial task.

"Haymaking is a good example," he told me, not long into one of our conversations on the topic. "It's a subject where I can give you the basic idea without having to gloss over the underlying economics."

When Pritchard took over Smith Meadows, he explained, the farm made its own hay to use as animal feed during the winter months when grazing is impossible. Haymaking is done with a piece of equipment called a hay baler: a device you pull behind a tractor that compresses and binds dried grass into bales. If you raise animals on the East Coast there's an obvious reason to own and operate a hay baler: Your animals need hay. Why spend money to "buy in" feed when you have perfectly good grass growing for free right in your own soil? If a farmer subscribed to the any-benefit approach used by knowledge workers, therefore, he would definitely buy a hay baler. But as Pritchard explained to me (after preemptively apologizing for a moment of snark), if a farmer actually adopted such a simplistic mind-set, "I'd be counting the days until the 'For Sale' sign goes up on the property." Pritchard, like most practitioners of his trade, instead deploys a more sophisticated thought process when assessing tools. And after applying this process to the hay baler, Pritchard was quick to sell it: Smith Meadows now purchases all the hay it uses.

Here's why . . .

"Let's start by exploring the costs of making hay," Pritchard said. "First, there's the actual cost of fuel, and repairs, and the shed to keep the baler. You also have to pay taxes on it." These directly measurable costs, however, were the easy part of his decision. It was instead the "opportunity costs" that required more attention. As he elaborated: "If I make hay all summer, I can't be doing something else. For example, I now use that time instead to raise boilers [chickens meant for eating]. These generate positive cash flow, because I can sell them. But they also produce manure which I can then use to enhance my soil." Then there's the equally subtle issue of assessing the secondary value of a purchased bale of hay. As Pritchard explained: "When I'm buying in hay, I'm trading cash for animal protein, as well as manure (once it passes through the animals' system), which means I am also getting more nutrients for my land in exchange for my money. I'm also avoiding compacting soils by driving heavy machinery over my ground all summer long."

When making his final decision on the baler, Pritchard moved past the direct monetary costs, which were essentially a wash, and instead shifted his attention to the more nuanced issue of the long-term health of his fields. For the reasons described previously, Pritchard concluded that buying in hay results in healthier fields. And as he summarized: "Soil fertility is my baseline." By this calculation, the baler had to go.

Notice the complexity of Pritchard's tool decision. This complexity underscores an important reality: The notion that identifying *some* benefit is sufficient to invest money, time, and attention in a tool is near laughable to people in his trade. *Of course* a hay baler offers benefits—*every* tool at the farm supply store has something useful to offer. At the same time, *of course* it offers negatives as well. Pritchard expected this decision to be nuanced. He began with a clear baseline—in his case, that soil health is of fundamental importance to his professional success—and then built off this foundation toward a final call on whether to use a particular tool.

I propose that if you're a knowledge worker—especially one interested in cultivating a deep work habit—you should treat your tool selection with the same level of care as other skilled workers, such as farmers. Following is my attempt to generalize this assessment strategy. I call it the *craftsman approach* to tool selection, a name that emphasizes that tools are ultimately aids to the larger goals of one's craft.

The Craftsman Approach to Tool Selection: Identify the core factors that determine success and happiness in your professional and personal life. Adopt a tool only if its positive impacts on these factors substantially outweigh its negative impacts.

Notice that this craftsman approach to tool selection stands in opposition to the any-benefit approach. Whereas the any-benefit mind-set identifies any potential positive impact as justification for using a tool, the craftsman variant requires that these positive impacts affect factors at the core of what's important to you and that they outweigh the negatives.

Even though the craftsman approach rejects the simplicity of the any-benefit approach, it doesn't ignore the benefits that currently drive people to network tools, or make any advance proclamations about what's "good" or "bad" technology: It simply asks that you give any particular network tool the same type of measured, nuanced accounting that tools in other trades have been subjected to throughout the history of skilled labor.

The three strategies that follow in this rule are designed to grow your comfort with abandoning the any-benefit mindset and instead applying the more thoughtful craftsman philosophy in curating the tools that lay claim to your time and attention. This guidance is important because the craftsman approach is not cut-and-dry. Identifying what matters most in your life, and then attempting to assess the impacts of various tools on these factors, doesn't reduce to a simple formula—this task requires practice and experimentation. The strategies that follow provide some structure for this practice and experimentation by forcing you to reconsider your network tools from many different angles. Combined, they should help you cultivate a more sophisticated relationship with your tools that will allow you to take back enough control over your time and attention to enable the rest of the ideas in Part 2 to succeed.

Apply the Law of the Vital Few to Your Internet Habits

Malcolm Gladwell doesn't use Twitter. In a 2013 interview he explained why: "Who says my fans want to hear from me on Twitter?" He then joked: "I know a lot of people would like to see less of me." Michael Lewis, another mega-bestselling author, also doesn't use the service, explaining in The Wire: "I don't tweet, I don't Twitter, I couldn't even tell you how to read or where to find a Twitter message." And as mentioned in Part 1, the award-winning *New Yorker* scribe George Packer also avoids the service, and indeed only recently even succumbed to the necessity of owning a smartphone.

These three writers don't think Twitter is useless. They're quick to accept that other writers find it useful. Packer's admission of non-Twitter use, in fact, was written as a response to an unabashedly pro-Twitter article by the late *New York Times* media critic David Carr, a piece in which Carr effused:

> *And now, nearly a year later, has Twitter turned my brain to mush? No, I'm in narrative on more things in a given moment than I ever thought possible, and instead of spending a half-hour surfing in search of illumination, I get a sense of the day's news and how people are reacting to it in the time that it takes to wait for coffee at Starbucks.*

At the same time, however, Gladwell, Lewis, and Packer don't feel like the service offers them nearly enough advantages to offset its negatives in their particular circumstances. Lewis, for example, worries that adding more accessibility will sap his energy and reduce his ability to research and write great stories, noting: "It's amazing how overly accessible people are. There's a lot of communication in my life that's not enriching, it's impoverishing." While Packer, for his part, worries about distraction, saying: "Twitter is crack for media addicts." He goes so far as to describe Carr's rave about the service as "the most frightening picture of the future that I've read thus far in the new decade."

We don't have to argue about whether these authors are right in their personal decisions to avoid Twitter (and similar tools), because their sales numbers and awards speak for themselves. We can instead use these decisions as a courageous illustration of the craftsman approach to tool selection in action. In a time when so many knowledge workers—and especially those in creative fields—are still trapped in the any-benefit mind-set, it's refreshing to see a more mature approach to sorting through such services. But the very rareness of these examples reminds us that mature and confident assessments of this type aren't easy to make. Recall the complexity of the thought process, highlighted earlier, that Forrest Pritchard had to slog through to make a decision on his hay baler: For many knowledge workers, and many of the tools in their lives, these decisions will be equally complex. The goal of this strategy, therefore, is to offer some structure to this thought process—a way to reduce some of the complexity of deciding which tools really matter to you.

The first step of this strategy is to identify the main high-level goals in both your professional and your personal life. If you have a family, for example, then your personal goals might involve parenting well and running an organized household. In the professional sphere, the details of these goals depend on what you do for a living. In my own work as a professor, for example, I pursue two important goals, one centered on being an effective teacher in the classroom and effective mentor to my graduate students, and another centered on being an effective researcher. While your goals will likely differ, the key is to keep the list limited to what's most important and to keep the descriptions suitably high-level. (If your goal includes a specific target—"to reach a million dollars in sales" or "to publish a half dozen papers in a single year"—then it's too specific for our purposes here.) When you're done you should have a small number of goals for both the personal and professional areas of your life.

Once you've identified these goals, list for each the two or three most important activities that help you satisfy the goal. These activities should be specific enough to allow you to clearly picture doing them. On the other hand, they should be general enough that they're not tied to a onetime outcome. For example, "do better research" is too general (what does it look like to be "doing better research"?), while "finish paper on broadcast lower bounds in time for upcoming conference submission" is too specific (it's a onetime outcome). A good activity in this context would be something like: "regularly read and understand the cutting-edge results in my field."

The next step in this strategy is to consider the network tools you currently use. For each such tool, go through the key activities you identified and ask whether the use of the tool has a *substantially positive impact*, a *substantially negative impact*, or *little impact* on your regular and successful participation in the activity. Now comes the important decision: Keep using this tool only if you concluded that it has substantial positive impacts and that these outweigh the negative impacts.

To help illustrate this strategy in action, let's consider a case study. For the purposes of this example, assume that

Michael Lewis, if asked, would have produced the following goal and corresponding important activities for his writing career.

<u>Professional Goal</u>: To craft well-written, narrative-driven stories that change the way people understand the world.

<u>Key Activities Supporting This Goal</u>:
- Research patiently and deeply.
- Write carefully and with purpose.

Now imagine that Lewis was using this goal to determine whether or not to use Twitter. Our strategy requires him to investigate Twitter's impact on the key activities he listed that support his goal. There's no convincing way to argue that Twitter would make Lewis substantially better at either of these activities. Deep research for Lewis, I assume, requires him to spend weeks and months getting to know a small number of sources (he's a master of the long-form journalism skill of drawing out a source's story over many sessions), and careful writing, of course, requires freedom from distraction. In both cases, Twitter at best has no real impact, and at worst could be substantially negative, depending on Lewis's susceptibility to the service's addictive attributes. The conclusion would therefore be that Lewis shouldn't use Twitter.

You might argue at this point that confining our example to this single goal is artificial, as it ignores the areas where a service like Twitter has its best chance of contributing. For writers, in particular, Twitter is often presented as a tool to establish connections with your audience that ultimately lead to more sales. For a writer like Michael Lewis, however, marketing doesn't likely merit its own goal when he assesses what's important in his professional life. This follows because his reputation guarantees that he will receive massive coverage in massively influential media channels, *if* the book is really good. His focus, therefore, is much more productively applied to the goal of writing the best possible book than instead trying to squeeze out a few extra sales through inefficient author-driven means. In other words, the question is not whether Twitter has some conceivable benefit to Lewis; it's instead whether Twitter use significantly and positively affects the most important activities in his professional life.

What about a less famous writer? In this case, book marketing might play a more primary role in his or her goals. But when forced to identify the two or three most important activities supporting this goal, it's unlikely that the type of lightweight one-on-one contact enabled by Twitter would make the list. This is the result of simple math. Imagine that our hypothetical author diligently sends ten individualized tweets a day, five days a week—each of which connects one-on-one with a new potential reader. Now imagine that 50 percent of the people contacted in this manner become loyal fans who will definitely buy the author's next book. Over the two-year period it might take to write this book, this yields two thousand sales—a modest boost at best in a marketplace where bestseller status requires two or three times more sales *per week*. The question once again is not whether Twitter offers *some* benefits, but instead whether it offers *enough* benefits to offset its drag on your time and attention (two resources that are especially valuable to a writer).

Having seen an example of this approach applied to a professional context, let's next consider the potentially more disruptive setting of personal goals. In particular, let's apply this approach to one of our culture's most ubiquitous and fiercely defended tools: Facebook.

When justifying the use of Facebook (or similar social networks), most people cite its importance to their social lives. With this in mind, let's apply our strategy to understand whether Facebook makes the cut due to its positive impact on this aspect of our personal goals. To do so, we'll once again work with a hypothetical goal and key supporting activities.

Personal Goal: To maintain close and rewarding friendships with a group of people who are important to me.

Key Activities Supporting This Goal:
1. Regularly take the time for meaningful connection with those who are most important to me (e.g., a long talk, a meal, joint activity).
2. Give of myself to those who are most important to me (e.g., making nontrivial sacrifices that improve their lives).

Not everyone will share this exact goal or supporting activities, but hopefully you'll stipulate that they apply to many people. Let's now step back and apply our strategy's filtering logic to the example of Facebook in the context of this personal goal. This service, of course, offers any number of benefits to your social life. To name a few that are often mentioned: It allows you to catch up with people you haven't seen in a while, it allows you to maintain lightweight contact with people you know but don't run into regularly, it allows you to more easily monitor important events in people's lives (such as whether or not they're married or what their new baby looks like), and it allows you to stumble onto online communities or groups that match your interests.

These are real benefits that Facebook undeniably offers, but none of these benefits provide a significant positive impact to the two key activities we listed, both of which are offline and effort intensive. Our strategy, therefore, would return a perhaps surprising but clear conclusion: *Of course Facebook offers benefits to your social life, but none are important enough to what really matters to you in this area to justify giving it access to your time and attention.**

To be clear, I'm not arguing that everyone should stop using Facebook. I'm instead showing that for this specific (representative) case study, the strategy proposed here would suggest dropping this service. I can imagine, however, other plausible scenarios that would lead to the opposite

---

* It was exactly this type of analysis that supports my own lack of presence on Facebook. I've never been a member and I've undoubtedly missed out on many minor benefits of the type summarized above, but this hasn't affected my quest to maintain a thriving and rewarding social life to any noticeable degree.

conclusion. Consider, for example, a college freshman. For someone in this situation, it might be more important to establish new friendships than to support existing relationships. The activities this student identifies for supporting his goal of a thriving social life, therefore, might include something like, "attend lots of events and socialize with lots of different people." If this is a key activity, and you're on a college campus, then a tool like Facebook would have a substantially positive impact and *should be used*.

To give another example, consider someone in the military who's deployed overseas. For this hypothetical soldier, keeping in frequent lightweight touch with friends and family left back home is a plausible priority, and one that might once again be best supported through social networks.

What should be clear from these examples is that this strategy, if applied as described, will lead many people who currently use tools like Facebook or Twitter to abandon them—but not everyone. You might, at this point, complain about the arbitrariness of allowing only a small number of activities to dominate your decisions about such tools. As we established previously, for example, Facebook has many benefits to your social life; why would one abandon it just because it doesn't happen to help the small number of activities that we judged most important? What's key to understand here, however, is that this radical reduction of priorities is not arbitrary, but is instead motivated by an idea that has arisen repeatedly in any number of different fields, from client profitability to social equality to prevention of crashes in computer programs.

The Law of the Vital Few*: In many settings, 80 percent of a given effect is due to just 20 percent of the possible causes.

For example, it might be the case that 80 percent of a business's profits come from just 20 percent of its clients, 80 percent of a nation's wealth is held by its richest 20 percent of citizens, or 80 percent of computer software crashes come from just 20 percent of the identified bugs. There's a formal mathematical underpinning to this phenomenon (an 80/20 split is roughly what you would expect when describing a *power law* distribution over impact—a type of distribution that shows up often when measuring quantities in the real world), but it's probably most useful when applied heuristically as a reminder that, in many cases, contributions to an outcome are not evenly distributed.

Moving forward, let's assume that this law holds for the important goals in your life. As we noted, many different activities can contribute to your achieving these goals. The law of the vital few, however, reminds us that the most important 20 percent or so of these activities provide the bulk of the benefit. Assuming that you could probably list somewhere between ten and fifteen distinct and potentially beneficial activities for each of your life goals, this law says that it's the top two or three such activities—the number

---

* This idea has many different forms and names, including the 80/20 rule, Pareto's principle, and, if you're feeling particularly pretentious, the principle of factor sparsity.

that this strategy asks you to focus on—that make most of the difference in whether or not you succeed with the goal.

Even if you accept this result, however, you still might argue that you shouldn't ignore the other 80 percent of possible beneficial activities. It's true that these less important activities don't contribute nearly as much to your goal as your top one or two, but they can provide *some* benefit, so why not keep them in the mix? As long as you don't ignore the more important activities, it seems like it can't hurt to also support some of the less important alternatives.

This argument, however, misses the key point that all activities, regardless of their importance, consume your same limited store of time and attention. If you service low-impact activities, therefore, you're taking away time you could be spending on higher-impact activities. It's a zero-sum game. And because your time returns substantially more rewards when invested in high-impact activities than when invested in low-impact activities, the more of it you shift to the latter, the lower your overall benefit.

The business world understands this math. This is why it's not uncommon to see a company *fire* unproductive clients. If 80 percent of their profits come from 20 percent of their clients, then they make more money by redirecting the energy from low-revenue clients to better service the small number of lucrative contracts—each hour spent on the latter returns more revenue than each hour spent on the former. The same holds true for your professional and personal goals. By taking the time consumed by low-impact activities—like finding old friends on Facebook—and reinvesting in high-impact activities—like taking a good friend out to lunch—you end up more successful in your goal. To abandon a network tool using this logic, therefore, is not to miss out on its potential small benefits, but is instead to get more out of the activities you already know to yield large benefits.

To return to where we started, for Malcolm Gladwell, Michael Lewis, and George Packer, Twitter doesn't support the 20 percent of activities that generate the bulk of the success in their writing careers. Even though in isolation this service might return some minor benefits, when their careers are viewed as a whole, they're likely more successful not using Twitter, and redirecting that time to more fruitful activities, than if they added it into their schedule as one more thing to manage. You should take this same care in deciding which tools you allow to claim your own limited time and attention.

Quit Social Media

When Ryan Nicodemus decided to simplify his life, one of his first targets was his possessions. At the time, Ryan lived alone in a spacious three-bedroom condo. For years, driven by a consumerist impulse, he had been trying his best to fill this ample space. Now it was time to reclaim his life from his stuff. The strategy he deployed was simple to describe but radical in concept. He spent an afternoon packing everything he owned into cardboard boxes as if he was about to move. In order to transform what he described as a "difficult undertaking" into something less onerous, he called it a "packing party," explaining: "Everything's more exciting when it's a party, right?"

Once the packing was done, Nicodemus then spent the next week going through his normal routine. If he needed something that was packed, he would unpack it and put it back where it used to go. At the end of the week, he noticed that the vast majority of his stuff remained untouched in its boxes.

So he got rid of it.

Stuff accumulates in people's lives, in part, because when faced with a specific act of elimination it's easy to worry, "What if I need this one day?," and then use this worry as an excuse to keep the item in question sitting around. Nicodemus's packing party provided him with definitive evidence that most of his stuff *was not* something he needed, and it therefore supported his quest to simplify.

The last strategy provided a systematic method to help you begin sorting through the network tools that currently lay claim to your time and attention. This strategy offers you a different but complementary approach to these same issues, and it's inspired by Ryan Nicodemus's approach to getting rid of his useless stuff.

In more detail, this strategy asks that you perform the equivalent of a packing party on the social media services that you currently use. Instead of "packing," however, you'll instead ban yourself from using them for *thirty days*. All of them: Facebook, Instagram, Google+, Twitter, Snapchat, Vine—or whatever other services have risen to popularity since I first wrote these words. Don't formally deactivate these services, and (this is important) don't mention online that you'll be signing off: Just stop using them, cold turkey. If someone reaches out to you by other means and asks why your activity on a particular service has fallen off, you can explain, but don't go out of your way to tell people.

After thirty days of this self-imposed network isolation, ask yourself the following two questions about each of the services you temporarily quit:

1. Would the last thirty days have been notably better if I had been able to use this service?
2. Did people care that I wasn't using this service?

If your answer is "no" to both questions, quit the service permanently. If your answer was a clear "yes," then return to using the service. If your answers are qualified or ambiguous, it's up to you whether you return to the service, though I would encourage you to lean toward quitting. (You can always rejoin later.)

This strategy picks specifically on social media because among the different network tools that can claim your time and attention, these services, if used without limit, can be particularly devastating to your quest to work deeper. They offer personalized information arriving on an unpredictable intermittent schedule—making them massively addictive and therefore capable of severely damaging your attempts to schedule and succeed with any act of concentration. Given these dangers, you might expect that more knowledge workers would avoid these tools altogether—especially those like computer programmers or writers whose livelihood explicitly depends on the outcome of deep work. But part of what makes social media insidious is that the companies that profit from your attention have succeeded with a masterful marketing coup: convincing our culture that if you don't use their products you might *miss out*.

This fear that you might miss out has obvious parallels to Nicodemus's fear that the voluminous stuff in his closets might one day prove useful, which is why I'm suggesting a corrective strategy that parallels his packing party. By spending a month without these services, you can replace your fear that you might miss out—on events, on conversations, on shared cultural experience—with a dose of reality. For most people this reality will confirm something that seems obvious only once you've done the hard work of freeing yourself from the marketing messages surrounding these tools: They're not really all that important in your life.

The reason why I ask you to not announce your thirty-day experiment is because for some people another part of the delusion that binds them to social media is the idea that people *want to hear what you have to say*, and that they might be disappointed if you suddenly leave them bereft of your commentary. I'm being somewhat facetious here in my wording, but this underlying sentiment is nonetheless common and important to tackle. As of this writing, for example, the average number of followers for a Twitter user is 208. When you know that more than two hundred people *volunteered* to hear what you have to say, it's easy to begin to believe that your activities on these services are important. Speaking from experience as someone who makes a living trying to sell my ideas to people: This is a powerfully addictive feeling!

But here's the reality of audiences in a social media era. Before these services existed, building an audience of any size beyond your immediate friends and family required hard, competitive work. In the early 2000s, for example, anyone could start a blog, but to gain even just a handful of unique visitors per month required that you actually put in the work to deliver information that's valuable enough to capture someone's attention. I know this difficulty well. My first blog was started in the fall of 2003. It was called, cleverly enough, *Inspiring Moniker*. I used it to muse on my life as a twenty-one-year-old college student. There were, I'm embarrassed to admit, long stretches where *no one* read it (a term I'm using literally). As I learned in the decade that followed, a period in which I patiently and painstakingly built an audience for my current blog, *Study Hacks*, from a handful of readers to hundreds of thousands per month, is that earning people's attention online is hard, hard work.

Except now it's not.

Part of what fueled social media's rapid assent, I contend, is its ability to short-circuit this connection between the hard work of producing real value and the positive reward of having people pay attention to you. It has instead replaced this timeless capitalist exchange with a shallow collectivist alternative: *I'll pay attention to what you say if you pay attention to what I say—regardless of its value.* A blog or magazine or television program that contained the content that typically populates a Facebook wall or Twitter feed, for example, would attract, on average, *no* audience. But when captured within the social conventions of these services, that same content will attract attention in the form of likes and comments. The implicit agreement motivating this behavior is that in return for receiving (for the most part, undeserved) attention from your friends and followers, you'll return the favor by lavishing (similarly undeserved) attention on them. *You "like" my status update and I'll "like" yours.* This agreement gives everyone a simulacrum of importance without requiring much effort in return.

By dropping off these services without notice you can test the reality of your status as a content producer. For most people and most services, the news might be sobering—no one outside your closest friends and family will likely even notice you've signed off. I recognize that I come across as curmudgeonly when talking about this issue—is there any other way to tackle it?—but it's important to discuss because this quest for self-importance plays an important role in convincing people to continue to thoughtlessly fragment their time and attention.

For some people, of course, this thirty-day experiment will be difficult and generate lots of issues. If you're a college student or online personality, for example, the abstention will complicate your life and will be noted. But for most, I suspect, the net result of this experiment, if not a massive overhaul in your Internet habits, will be a more grounded view of the role social media plays in your daily existence.

These services aren't necessarily, as advertised, the lifeblood of our modern connected world. They're just products, developed by private companies, funded lavishly, marketed carefully, and designed ultimately to capture then sell your personal information and attention to advertisers. They can be fun, but in the scheme of your life and what you want to accomplish, they're a lightweight whimsy, one unimportant distraction among many threatening to derail you from something deeper. Or maybe social media tools are at the core of your existence. You won't know either way until you sample life without them.

Don't Use the Internet to Entertain Yourself

Arnold Bennett was an English writer born near the turn of the twentieth century—a tumultuous time for his home country's economy. The industrial revolution, which had been roaring for decades by this point, had wrenched enough surplus capital from the empire's resources to generate a new class: the white-collar worker. It was now possible to have a job in which you spent a set number of hours a week in an office, and in exchange received a steady salary sufficient to support a household. Such a lifestyle is blandly familiar in our current age, but to Bennett and his contemporaries it was novel and in many ways distressing. Chief among Bennett's concerns was that members of this new class were missing out on the opportunities it presented to live a full life.

"Take the case of a Londoner who works in an office, whose office hours are from ten to six, and who spends fifty minutes morning and night in travelling between his house door and his office door," Bennett writes in his 1910 self-help classic, *How to Live on 24 Hours a Day*. This hypothetical London salaryman, he notes, has a little more than sixteen hours left in the day beyond these work-related hours. To Bennett, this is a lot of time, but most people in this situation tragically don't realize its potential. The "great and profound mistake which my typical man makes in regard to his day," he elaborates, is that even though he doesn't particularly enjoy his work (seeing it as something to "get through"), "he persists in looking upon those hours from ten to six as 'the day,' to which the ten hours preceding them and the six hours following them are nothing but a prologue and epilogue." This is an attitude that Bennett condemns as "utterly illogical and unhealthy."

What's the alternative to this state of affairs? Bennett suggests that his typical man see his sixteen free hours as a "day within a day," explaining, "during those sixteen hours he is free; he is not a wage-earner; he is not preoccupied with monetary cares; he is just as good as a man with a private income." Accordingly, the typical man should instead use this time as an aristocrat would: to perform rigorous self-improvement—a task that, according to Bennett, involves, primarily, reading great literature and poetry.

Bennett wrote about these issues more than a century ago. You might expect that in the intervening decades, a period in which this middle class exploded in size worldwide, our thinking about leisure time would have evolved. But it has not. If anything, with the rise of the Internet and the low-brow attention economy it supports, the average forty-hour-a-week employee—especially those in my tech-savvy Millennial generation—has seen the quality of his or her leisure time remain degraded, consisting primarily of a blur of distracted clicks on least-common-denominator digital entertainment. If Bennett were brought back to life today, he'd likely fall into despair at the lack of progress in this area of human development.

To be clear, I'm indifferent to the moral underpinnings behind Bennett's suggestions. His vision of elevating the souls and minds of the middle class by reading poetry and great books feels somewhat antiquated and classist. But the logical foundation of his proposal, that you both *should* and *can* make deliberate use of your time outside work, remains relevant today—especially with respect to the goal of this rule, which is to reduce the impact of network tools on your ability to perform deep work.

In more detail, in the strategies discussed so far in this rule, we haven't spent much time yet on a class of network tools that are particularly relevant to the fight for depth: entertainment-focused websites designed to capture and hold your attention for as long as possible. At the time of this writing, the most popular examples of such sites include the Huffington Post, BuzzFeed, Business Insider, and Reddit. This list will undoubtedly continue to evolve, but what this general category of sites shares is the use of carefully crafted titles and easily digestible content, often honed by algorithms to be maximally attention catching.

Once you've landed on one article in one of these sites,

links on the side or bottom of the page beckon you to click on another, then another. Every available trick of human psychology, from listing titles as "popular" or "trending," to the use of arresting photos, is used to keep you engaged. At this particular moment, for example, some of the most popular articles on BuzzFeed include, "17 Words That Mean Something Totally Different When Spelled Backward" and "33 Dogs Winning at Everything."

These sites are especially harmful after the workday is over, where the freedom in your schedule enables them to become central to your leisure time. If you're waiting in line, or waiting for the plot to pick up in a TV show, or waiting to finish eating a meal, they provide a cognitive crutch to ensure you eliminate any chance of boredom. As I argued in Rule #2, however, such behavior is dangerous, as it weakens your mind's general ability to resist distraction, making deep work difficult later when you really want to concentrate. To make matters worse, these network tools are not something you join and therefore they're not something you can remove from your life by quitting (rendering the previous two strategies irrelevant). They're always available, just a quick click away.

Fortunately, Arnold Bennett identified the solution to this problem a hundred years earlier: *Put more thought into your leisure time.* In other words, this strategy suggests that when it comes to your relaxation, don't default to whatever catches your attention at the moment, but instead dedicate some advance thinking to the question of how you want to spend your "day within a day." Addictive websites of the type mentioned previously thrive in a vacuum: If you haven't given yourself something to do in a given moment, they'll always beckon as an appealing option. If you instead fill this free time with something of more quality, their grip on your attention will loosen.

It's crucial, therefore, that you figure out in advance what you're going to do with your evenings and weekends before they begin. Structured hobbies provide good fodder for these hours, as they generate specific actions with specific goals to fill your time. A set program of reading, à la Bennett, where you spend regular time each night making progress on a series of deliberately chosen books, is also a good option, as is, of course, exercise or the enjoyment of good (in-person) company.

In my own life, for example, I manage to read a surprising number of books in a typical year, given the demands on my time as a professor, writer, and father (on average, I'm typically reading three to five books at a time). This is possible because one of my favorite preplanned leisure activities after my kids' bedtime is to read an interesting book. As a result, my smartphone and computer, and the distractions they can offer, typically remain neglected between the end of the workday and the next morning.

At this point you might worry that adding such structure to your relaxation will defeat the purpose of relaxing, which many believe requires complete freedom from plans or obligations. Won't a structured evening leave you exhausted—not refreshed—the next day at work? Bennett, to his credit, anticipated this complaint. As he argues, such worries misunderstand what energizes the human spirit:

What? You say that full energy given to those sixteen hours will lessen the value of the business eight? Not so. On the contrary, it will assuredly increase the value of the business eight. One of the chief things which my typical man has to learn is that the mental faculties are capable of a continuous hard activity; they do not tire like an arm or a leg. All they want is change—not rest, except in sleep.

In my experience, this analysis is spot-on. If you give your mind something meaningful to do throughout *all* your waking hours, you'll end the day more fulfilled, and begin the next one more relaxed, than if you instead allow your mind to bathe for hours in semiconscious and unstructured Web surfing.

To summarize, if you want to eliminate the addictive pull of entertainment sites on your time and attention, give your brain a quality alternative. Not only will this preserve your ability to resist distraction and concentrate, but you might even fulfill Arnold Bennett's ambitious goal of experiencing, perhaps for the first time, what it means to live, and not just exist.

Rule #4

Drain the Shallows

In the summer of 2007, the software company 37signals (now called Basecamp) launched an experiment: They shortened their workweek from five days to four. Their employees seemed to accomplish the same amount of work with one less day, so they made this change permanent: Every year, from May through October, 37signals employees work only Monday to Thursday (with the exception of customer support, which still operates the full week). As company cofounder Jason Fried quipped in a blog post about the decision: "People should enjoy the weather in the summer."

It didn't take long before the grumbles began in the business press. A few months after Fried announced his company's decision to make four-day weeks permanent, journalist Tara Weiss wrote a critical piece for *Forbes* titled "Why a Four-Day Work Week Doesn't Work." She summarized her problem with this strategy as follows:

> *Packing 40 hours into four days isn't necessarily an effi-cient way to work. Many people find that eight hours*

are tough enough; requiring them to stay for an extra
two could cause morale and productivity to decrease.

Fried was quick to respond. In a blog post titled "Forbes
Misses the Point of the 4-Day Work Week," he begins by
agreeing with Weiss's premise that it *would* be stressful for
employees to cram forty hours of effort into four days. But,
as he clarifies, that's not what he's suggesting. "The point
of the 4-day work week is about *doing less work*," he writes.
"It's not about four 10-hour days ... it's about four normalish
8-hour days."

This might seem confusing at first. Fried earlier claimed
that his employees get just as much done in four days as in
five days. Now, however, he's claiming that his employees
are working fewer hours. How can both be true? The difference, it turns out, concerns the role of shallow work. As
Fried expands:

> *Very few people work even 8 hours a day. You're lucky*
> *if you get a few good hours in between all the meetings,*
> *interruptions, web surfing, office politics, and personal*
> *business that permeate the typical workday.*
>
> *Fewer official working hours helps squeeze the fat*
> *out of the typical workweek. Once everyone has less*
> *time to get their stuff done, they respect that time even*
> *more. People become stingy with their time and that's a*
> *good thing. They don't waste it on things that just don't*
> *matter. When you have fewer hours you usually spend*
> *them more wisely.*

In other words, the reduction in the 37signals workweek disproportionately eliminated shallow as compared to deep work, and because the latter was left largely untouched, the important stuff continued to get done. The shallow stuff that can seem so urgent in the moment turned out to be unexpectedly dispensable.

A natural reaction to this experiment is to wonder what would happen if 37signals had gone one step further. If eliminating hours of shallow work had little impact on the results produced, what would happen if they not only eliminated shallow work, but then replaced this newly recovered time with more deep work? Fortunately for our curiosity, the company soon put this bolder idea to the test as well.

Fried had always been interested in the policies of technology companies like Google that gave their employees 20 percent of their time to work on self-directed projects. While he liked this idea, he felt that carving one day out of an otherwise busy week was not enough to support the type of unbroken deep work that generates true breakthroughs. "I'd take 5 days in a row over 5 days spread out over 5 weeks," he explained. "So our theory is that we'll see better results when people have a long stretch of uninterrupted time."

To test this theory, 37signals implemented something radical: The company gave its employees the *entire month of June* off to work deeply on their own projects. This month would be a period free of any shallow work obligations—no status meetings, no memos, and, blessedly, no PowerPoint. At the end of the month, the company held a "pitch day" in which employees pitched the ideas they'd been working on. Summarizing the experiment in an *Inc.* magazine article, Fried dubbed it a success. The pitch day produced two projects that were soon put into production: a better suite of tools for handling customer support and a data visualization system that helps the company understand how their customers use their products. These projects are predicted to bring substantial value to the company, but they almost certainly would *not* have been produced in the absence of the unobstructed deep work time provided to the employees. To tease out their potential required dozens of hours of unimpeded effort.

"How can we afford to put our business on hold for a month to 'mess around' with new ideas?" Fried asked rhetorically. "How can we afford not to?"

———————

37signals' experiments highlight an important reality: The shallow work that increasingly dominates the time and attention of knowledge workers is less vital than it often seems in the moment. For most businesses, if you eliminated significant amounts of this shallowness, their bottom line would likely remain unaffected. And as Jason Fried discovered, if you not only eliminate shallow work, but also replace this recovered time with more of the deep alternative, not only will the business continue to function; it can become *more* successful.

This rule asks you to apply these insights to your personal work life. The strategies that follow are designed to help you ruthlessly identify the shallowness in your current schedule, then cull it down to minimum levels—leaving more time for the deep efforts that ultimately matter most.

Before diving into the details of these strategies, however, we should first confront the reality that there's a limit to this anti-shallow thinking. The value of deep work vastly outweighs the value of shallow, but this doesn't mean that you must quixotically pursue a schedule in which *all* of your time is invested in depth. For one thing, a nontrivial amount of shallow work is needed to maintain most knowledge work jobs. You might be able to avoid checking your e-mail every ten minutes, but you won't likely last long if you *never* respond to important messages. In this sense, we should see the goal of this rule as taming shallow work's footprint in your schedule, not eliminating it.

Then there's the issue of cognitive capacity. Deep work is exhausting because it pushes you toward the limit of your abilities. Performance psychologists have extensively studied how much such efforts can be sustained by an individual in a given day.* In their seminal paper on deliberate practice, Anders Ericsson and his collaborators survey these studies. They note that for someone new to such practice (citing, in particular, a child in the early stages of developing an expert-level skill), an hour a day is a reasonable limit. For those

---

* The studies I cite are looking at the activity of deliberate practice—which substantially (but not completely) overlaps our definition of deep work. For our purposes here, deliberate practice is a good specific stand-in for the general category of cognitively demanding tasks to which deep work belongs.

familiar with the rigors of such activities, the limit expands to something like four hours, but rarely more.

The implication is that once you've hit your deep work limit in a given day, you'll experience diminishing rewards if you try to cram in more. Shallow work, therefore, doesn't become dangerous until after you add enough to begin to crowd out your bounded deep efforts for the day. At first, this caveat might seem optimistic. The typical workday is eight hours. The most adept deep thinker cannot spend more than four of these hours in a state of true depth. It follows that you can safely spend half the day wallowing in the shallows without adverse effect. The danger missed by this analysis is how *easily* this amount of time can be consumed, especially once you consider the impact of meetings, appointments, calls, and other scheduled events. For many jobs, these time drains can leave you with surprisingly little time left for solo work.

My job as a professor, for example, is traditionally less plagued by such commitments, but even so, they often take large chunks out of my time, especially during the academic year. Turning to a random day in my calendar from the previous semester (I'm writing this during a quiet summer month), for example, I see I had a meeting from eleven to twelve, another from one to two thirty, and a class to teach from three to five. My eight-hour workday in this example is already reduced by four hours. Even if I squeezed all remaining shallow work (e-mails, tasks) into a single half hour, I'd still fall short of the goal of four hours of daily deep work. Put another way, even though we're not capable of spending a full day in a state of blissful depth, this reality shouldn't reduce the urgency of reducing shallow work, as the typical knowledge workday is more easily fragmented than many suspect.

To summarize, I'm asking you to treat shallow work with suspicion because its damage is often vastly underestimated and its importance vastly overestimated. This type of work is inevitable, but you must keep it confined to a point where it doesn't impede your ability to take full advantage of the deeper efforts that ultimately determine your impact. The strategies that follow will help you act on this reality.

Schedule Every Minute of Your Day

If you're between the ages of twenty-five and thirty-four years old and live in Britain, you likely watch more television than you realize. In 2013, the British TV licensing authority surveyed television watchers about their habits. The twenty-five- to thirty-four-year-olds taking the survey estimated that they spend somewhere between fifteen and sixteen hours per week watching TV. This sounds like a lot, but it's actually a significant underestimate. We know this because when it comes to television-watching habits, we have access to the ground truth. The Broadcasters' Audience Research Board (the British equivalent of the American Nielsen Company) places meters in a representative sample of households. These meters record, without bias or wishful thinking, exactly how much people *actually* watch. The twenty-five- to thirty-four-year-olds who thought they watched fifteen hours a week, it turns out, watch more like twenty-eight hours.

This bad estimate of time usage is not unique to British television watching. When you consider different groups self-estimating different behaviors, similar gaps stubbornly remain. In a *Wall Street Journal* article on the topic, business writer Laura Vanderkam pointed out several more such examples. A survey by the National Sleep Foundation revealed that Americans think they're sleeping, on average, somewhere around seven hours a night. The American Time Use Survey, which has people actually measure their sleep, corrected this number to 8.6 hours. Another study found that people who claimed to work sixty to sixty-four hours per week were actually averaging more like forty-four hours per week, while those claiming to work more than seventy-five hours were actually working less than fifty-five.

These examples underscore an important point: We spend much of our day on autopilot—not giving much thought to what we're doing with our time. *This is a problem.* It's difficult to prevent the trivial from creeping into every corner of your schedule if you don't face, without flinching, your current balance between deep and shallow work, and then adopt the habit of pausing before action and asking, "What makes the most sense right now?" The strategy described in the following paragraphs is designed to force you into these behaviors. It's an idea that might seem extreme at first but will soon prove indispensable in your quest to take full advantage of the value of deep work: *Schedule every minute of your day.*

Here's my suggestion: At the beginning of each workday, turn to a new page of lined paper in a notebook you dedicate to this purpose. Down the left-hand side of the page, mark every other line with an hour of the day, covering the full set of hours you typically work. Now comes the important part: Divide the hours of your workday into *blocks* and assign activities to the blocks. For example, you might block off nine a.m. to eleven a.m. for writing a client's press release. To do so, actually draw a box that covers the lines corresponding to these hours, then write "press release" inside the box. Not every block need be dedicated to a work task. There might be time blocks for lunch or relaxation breaks. To keep things reasonably clean, the minimum length of a block should be thirty minutes (i.e., one line on your page). This means, for example, that instead of having a unique small box for each small task on your plate for the day—*respond to boss's e-mail, submit reimbursement form, ask Carl about report*—you can batch similar things into more generic *task blocks*. You might find it useful, in this case, to draw a line from a task block to the open right-hand side of the page where you can list out the full set of small tasks you plan to accomplish in that block.

When you're done scheduling your day, every minute should be part of a block. You have, in effect, given every minute of your workday a job. Now as you go through your day, use this schedule to guide you.

It's here, of course, that most people will begin to run into trouble. Two things can (and likely will) go wrong with your schedule once the day progresses. The first is that your estimates will prove wrong. You might put aside two hours for writing a press release, for example, and in reality it takes two and a half hours. The second problem is that you'll be interrupted and new obligations will unexpectedly appear on your plate. These events will also break your schedule.

This is okay. If your schedule is disrupted, you should, at the next available moment, take a few minutes to create a revised schedule for the time that remains in the day. You can turn to a new page. You can erase and redraw blocks. Or do as I do: Cross out the blocks for the remainder of the day and create new blocks to the right of the old ones on the page (I draw my blocks skinny so I have room for several revisions). On some days, you might rewrite your schedule half a dozen times. Don't despair if this happens. Your goal is not to stick to a given schedule at all costs; it's instead to maintain, at all times, a thoughtful say in what you're doing with your time going forward—even if these decisions are reworked again and again as the day unfolds.

If you find that schedule revisions become overwhelming in their frequency, there are a few tactics that can inject some more stability. First, you should recognize that *almost definitely* you're going to underestimate at first how much time you require for most things. When people are new to this habit, they tend to use their schedule as an incarnation of wishful thinking—a best-case scenario for their day. Over time, you should make an effort to accurately (if not somewhat conservatively) predict the time tasks will require.

The second tactic that helps is the use of *overflow conditional* blocks. If you're not sure how long a given activity might take, block off the expected time, then follow this with an additional block that has a split purpose. If you need more time for the preceding activity, use this additional block to keep working on it. If you finish the activity on time, however, have an alternate use already assigned for the extra block (for example, some nonurgent tasks). This allows unpredictability in your day without requiring you to keep changing your schedule on paper. For example, returning to our press release example, you might schedule two hours for writing the press release, but then follow it by an additional hour block that you can use to keep writing the release, if needed, but otherwise assign to catching up with e-mail.

The third tactic I suggest is to be liberal with your use of task blocks. Deploy many throughout your day and make them longer than required to handle the tasks you plan in the morning. Lots of things come up during the typical knowledge worker's day: Having regularly occurring blocks of time to address these surprises keeps things running smoothly.

Before leaving you to put this strategy in practice, I should address a common objection. In my experience pitching the values of daily schedules, I've found that many people worry that this level of planning will become burdensomely restrictive. Here, for example, is part of a comment from a reader named Joseph on a blog post I wrote on this topic:

I think you far understate the role of uncertainty...I [worry about] readers applying these observations too seriously, to the point of an obsessive (and unhealthy) relationship with one's schedule that seems to exaggerate the importance of minute-counting over getting-lost-in-activities, which if we're talking about artists is often the only really sensible course of action.

I understand these concerns, and Joseph is certainly not the first to raise them. Fortunately, however, they're also easily addressed. In my own daily scheduling discipline, in addition to regularly scheduling significant blocks of time for speculative thinking and discussion, I maintain a rule that if I stumble onto an important insight, then this is a perfectly valid reason to ignore the rest of my schedule for the day (with the exception, of course, of things that cannot be skipped). I can then stick with this unexpected insight until it loses steam. At this point, I'll step back and rebuild my schedule for any time that remains in the day.

In other words, I not only allow spontaneity in my schedule; I encourage it. Joseph's critique is driven by the mistaken idea that the goal of a schedule is to force your behavior into a rigid plan. This type of scheduling, however, isn't about constraint—it's instead about thoughtfulness. It's a simple habit that forces you to continually take a moment throughout your day and ask: "What makes sense for me to do with the time that remains?" It's the habit of asking that returns results, not your unyielding fidelity to the answer.

I would go so far as to argue that someone following this

combination of comprehensive scheduling and a willingness to adapt or modify the plan as needed will likely experience *more* creative insights than someone who adopts a more traditionally "spontaneous" approach where the day is left open and unstructured. Without structure, it's easy to allow your time to devolve into the shallow—e-mail, social media, Web surfing. This type of shallow behavior, though satisfying in the moment, is not conducive to creativity. With structure, on the other hand, you can ensure that you regularly schedule blocks to grapple with a new idea, or work deeply on something challenging, or brainstorm for a fixed period—the type of commitment more likely to instigate innovation. (Recall, for example, the discussion in Rule #1 about the rigid rituals followed by many great creative thinkers.) And because you're willing to abandon your plan when an innovative idea arises, you're just as well suited as the distracted creative to follow up when the muse strikes.

To summarize, the motivation for this strategy is the recognition that a deep work habit requires you to treat your time with respect. A good first step toward this respectful handling is the advice outlined here: Decide in advance what you're going to do with every minute of your workday. It's natural, at first, to resist this idea, as it's undoubtedly easier to continue to allow the twin forces of internal whim and external requests to drive your schedule. But you must overcome this distrust of structure if you want to approach your true potential as someone who creates things that matter.

Quantify the Depth of Every Activity

An advantage of scheduling your day is that you can determine how much time you're actually spending in shallow activities. Extracting this insight from your schedules, however, can become tricky in practice, as it's not always clear exactly how shallow you should consider a given task. To expand on this challenge, let's start by reminding ourselves of the formal definition of shallow work that I introduced in the introduction:

Shallow Work: Noncognitively demanding, logistical-style tasks, often performed while distracted. These efforts tend not to create much new value in the world and are easy to replicate.

Some activities clearly satisfy this definition. Checking e-mail, for example, or scheduling a conference call, is unquestionably shallow in nature. But the classification of other activities can be more ambiguous. Consider the following tasks:

- **Example #1**: Editing a draft of an academic article that you and a collaborator will soon submit to a journal.
- **Example #2**: Building a PowerPoint presentation about this quarter's sales figures.
- **Example #3**: Attending a meeting to discuss the current status of an important project and to agree on the next steps.

It's not obvious at first how to categorize these examples. The first two describe tasks that can be quite demanding, and the final example seems important to advance a key work objective. The purpose of this strategy is to give you an accurate metric for resolving such ambiguity—providing you with a way to make clear and consistent decisions about where given work tasks fall on the shallow-to-deep scale. To do so, it asks that you evaluate activities by asking a simple (but surprisingly illuminating) question:

> How long would it take (in months) to train a smart recent college graduate with no specialized training in my field to complete this task?

To illustrate this approach, let's apply this question to our examples of ambiguous tasks.

• **Analyzing Example #1**: To properly edit an academic paper requires that you understand the nuances of the work (so you can make sure it's being described precisely) and the nuances of the broader literature (so you can make sure it's being cited properly). These requirements require cutting-edge knowledge of an academic field—a task that in the age of specialization takes years of diligent study at the graduate level and beyond. When it comes to this example, the answer to our question would therefore be quite large, perhaps on the scale of fifty to seventy-five months.

- **Analyzing Example #2**: The second example doesn't fare so well by this analysis. To create a PowerPoint presentation that describes your quarterly sales requires three things: first, knowledge of how to make a PowerPoint presentation; second, an understanding of the standard format of these quarterly performance presentations within your organization; and third, an understanding of what sales metrics your organization tracks and how to convert them into the right graphs. The hypothetical college graduate imagined by our question, we can assume, would already know how to use PowerPoint, and learning the standard format for your organization's presentations shouldn't require more than a week. The real question, therefore, is how long it takes a bright college graduate to understand the metrics you track, where to find the results, and how to clean those up and translate them into graphs and charts that are appropriate for a slide presentation. This isn't a trivial task, but for a bright college grad it wouldn't require more than an additional month or so of training—so we can use two months as our conservative answer.

- **Analyzing Example #3**: Meetings can be tricky to analyze. They can seem tedious at times but they're often also presented as playing a key role in your organization's most important activities. The method presented here helps cut through this veneer. How long would it take to train a bright recent college graduate to take your place in a planning meeting? He or she would have to understand the project well enough to know its milestones and the skills of its participants. Our hypothetical grad might also need some insight into the interpersonal dynamics and the reality of how such projects are executed at the organization. At this point, you might wonder if this college grad would also need a deep expertise in the topic tackled by the project. For a planning meeting—probably not. Such meetings rarely dive into substantive content and tend to feature a lot of small talk and posturing in which participants try to make it seem like they're committing to a lot without actually having to commit. Give a bright recent graduate three months to learn the ropes and he or she could take your place without issue in such a gabfest. So we'll use three months as our answer.

This question is meant as a thought experiment (I'm not going to ask you to actually *hire* a recent college graduate to take over tasks that score low). But the answers it provides will help you objectively quantify the shallowness or depth of various activities. If our hypothetical college graduate requires many months of training to replicate a task, then this indicates that the task leverages hard-won expertise. As argued earlier, tasks that leverage your expertise tend to be deep tasks and they can therefore provide a double benefit: They return more value per time spent, and they stretch your abilities, leading to improvement. On the other hand, a task that our hypothetical college graduate can pick up quickly is one that does not leverage expertise, and therefore it can be understood as shallow.

What should you do with this strategy? Once you know where your activities fall on the deep-to-shallow scale, bias your time toward the former. When we reconsider our case studies, for example, we see that the first task is something that you would want to prioritize as a good use of time, while the second and third are activities of a type that should be minimized—they might feel productive, but their return on (time) investment is measly.

Of course, how one biases away from shallow and toward depth is not always obvious—even after you know how to accurately label your commitments. This brings us to the strategies that follow, which will provide specific guidance on how to accomplish this tricky goal.

Ask Your Boss for a Shallow Work Budget

Here's an important question that's rarely asked: *What percentage of my time should be spent on shallow work?* This strategy suggests that you ask it. If you have a boss, in other words, have a conversation about this question. (You'll probably have to first define for him or her what "shallow" and "deep" work means.) If you work for yourself, ask *yourself* this question. In both cases, settle on a specific answer. Then—and this is the important part—try to stick to this budget. (The strategies that precede and follow this one will help you achieve this goal.)

For most people in most non-entry-level knowledge work jobs, the answer to the question will be somewhere in the 30 to 50 percent range (there's a psychological distaste surrounding the idea of spending the *majority* of your time on unskilled tasks, so 50 percent is a natural upper limit, while at the same time most bosses will begin to worry that if this percentage gets too much lower than 30 percent you'll be reduced to a knowledge work hermit who thinks big thoughts but never responds to e-mails).

Obeying this budget will likely require changes to your behavior. You'll almost certainly end up forced into saying no to projects that seem infused with shallowness while also more aggressively reducing the amount of shallowness in your existing projects. This budget might lead you to drop the need for a weekly status meeting in preference for results-driven reporting ("let me know when you've made significant progress; then we'll talk"). It might also lead you to start spending more mornings in communication isolation or decide it's not as important as you once thought to respond quickly and in detail to every cc'd e-mail that crosses your inbox.

These changes are all positive for your quest to make deep work central to your working life. On the one hand, they don't ask you to abandon your core shallow obligations—a move that would cause problems and resentment—as you're still spending a lot of time on such efforts. On the other hand, they do force you to place a hard limit on the amount of less urgent obligations you allow to slip insidiously into your schedule. This limit frees up space for significant amounts of deep effort on a consistent basis.

The reason why these decisions should start with a conversation with your boss is that this agreement establishes implicit support from your workplace. If you work for someone else, this strategy provides cover when you turn down an obligation or restructure a project to minimize shallowness. You can justify the move because it's necessary for you to hit your prescribed target mix of work types. As I discussed in Chapter 2, part of the reason shallow work persists in large quantities in knowledge work is that we rarely see the total impact of such efforts on our schedules. We instead tend to evaluate these behaviors one by one in the moment—a perspective from which each task can seem quite reasonable and convenient. The tools from earlier in this rule, however, allow you to make this impact explicit. You can now confidently say to your boss, "This is the exact percentage of my time spent last week on shallow work," and force him or her to give explicit approval for that ratio. Faced with these numbers, and the economic reality they clarify (it's incredibly wasteful, for example, to pay a highly trained professional to send e-mail messages and attend meetings for thirty hours a week), a boss will be led to the natural conclusion that you *need* to say no to some things and to streamline others—even if this makes life less convenient for the boss, or for you, or for your coworkers. Because, of course, in the end, a business's goal is to generate value, not to make sure its employees' lives are as easy as possible.

If you work for yourself, this exercise will force you to confront the reality of how little time in your "busy" schedule you're actually producing value. These hard numbers will provide you the confidence needed to start scaling back on the shallow activities that are sapping your time. Without these numbers, it's difficult for an entrepreneur to say no to any opportunity that *might* generate some positive return. "I have to be on Twitter!," "I have to maintain an active Facebook presence!," "I have to tweak the widgets on my blog!," you tell yourself, because when considered in isolation, to say no to any one of these activities seems like you're being lazy. By instead picking and sticking with a shallow-to-deep ratio, you can replace this guilt-driven unconditional acceptance with the more healthy habit of trying to get the most out of the time you put aside for shallow work (therefore still exposing yourself to many opportunities), but keeping these efforts constrained to a small enough fraction of your time and attention to enable the deep work that ultimately drives your business forward.

Of course, there's always the possibility that when you ask this question the answer is stark. No boss will explicitly answer, "One hundred percent of your time should be shallow!" (unless you're entry level, at which point you need to delay this exercise until you've built enough skills to add deep efforts to your official work responsibilities), but a boss might reply, in so many words, "as much shallow work as is needed for you to promptly do whatever we need from you at the moment." In this case, the answer is still useful, as it tells you that this isn't a job that supports deep work, and a job that doesn't support deep work is not a job that can help you succeed in our current information economy. You should, in this case, thank the boss for the feedback, and then promptly start planning how you can transition into a new position that values depth.

Finish Your Work by Five Thirty

In the seven days preceding my first writing these words, I participated in sixty-five different e-mail conversations. Among these sixty-five conversations, I sent exactly five e-mails after five thirty p.m. The immediate story told by these statistics is that, with few exceptions, I don't send e-mails after five thirty. But given how intertwined e-mail has become with work in general, there's a more surprising reality hinted by this behavior: I don't *work* after five thirty p.m.

I call this commitment *fixed-schedule productivity*, as I fix the firm goal of not working past a certain time, then work backward to find productivity strategies that allow me to satisfy this declaration. I've practiced fixed-schedule productivity happily for more than half a decade now, and it's been crucial to my efforts to build a productive professional life centered on deep work. In the pages ahead, I will try to convince you to adopt this strategy as well.

———

Let me start my pitch for fixed-schedule productivity by first noting that, according to conventional wisdom, in the academic world I inhabit this tactic should fail. Professors—especially junior professors—are notorious for adopting grueling schedules that extend into the night and through weekends. Consider, for example, a blog post published by a young computer science professor whom I'll call "Tom." In this post, which Tom wrote in the winter of 2014, he replicates his schedule for a recent day in which he spent twelve hours at his office. This schedule includes five different meetings and three hours of "administrative" tasks, which he describes as "tending to bushels of e-mails, filling out bureaucratic forms, organizing meeting notes, planning future meetings." By his estimation, he spent only *one and a half* out of the twelve total hours sitting in his office tackling "real" work, which he defines as efforts that make progress toward a "research deliverable." It's no wonder that Tom feels coerced into working well beyond the standard workday. "I've already accepted the reality that I'll be working on weekends," he concludes in another post. "Very few junior faculty can avoid such a fate."

And yet, *I have*. Even though I don't work at night and rarely work on weekends, between arriving at Georgetown in the fall of 2011 and beginning work on this chapter in the fall of 2014, I've published somewhere around twenty peer-reviewed articles. I also won two competitive grants, published one (nonacademic) book, and have almost finished writing another (which you're reading at the moment). All while avoiding the grueling schedules deemed necessary by the Toms of the world.

What explains this paradox? We can find a compelling answer in a widely disseminated article published in 2013 by an academic further along in her career, and far more accomplished than I: Radhika Nagpal, the Fred Kavli Professor of Computer Science at Harvard University. Nagpal opens the article by claiming that much of the stress suffered by tenure-track professors is self-imposed. "Scary myths and scary data abound about life as a tenure-track faculty at an

'R1' [research-focused] university," she begins, before continuing to explain how she finally decided to disregard the conventional wisdom and instead "deliberately . . . do specific things to preserve my happiness." This deliberate effort led Nagpal to enjoy her pre-tenure time "tremendously."

Nagpal goes on to detail several examples of these efforts, but there's one tactic in particular that should sound familiar. As Nagpal admits, early in her academic career she found herself trying to cram work into every free hour between seven a.m. and midnight (because she has kids, this time, especially in the evening, was often severely fractured). It didn't take long before she decided this strategy was unsustainable, so she set a limit of fifty hours a week and worked backward to determine what rules and habits were needed to satisfy this constraint. Nagpal, in other words, deployed fixed-schedule productivity.

We know this strategy didn't hurt her academic career, as she ended up earning tenure on schedule and then jumping to the full professor level after only three additional years (an impressive ascent). How did she pull this off? According to her article, one of the main techniques for respecting her hour limit was to set drastic quotas on the major sources of *shallow* endeavors in her academic life. For example, she decided she would travel only five times per year for any purpose, as trips can generate a surprisingly large load of urgent shallow obligations (from making lodging arrangements to writing talks). Five trips a year may still sound like a lot, but for an academic it's light. To emphasize this point, note that Matt Welsh, a former colleague of Nagpal in the Harvard computer science department (he now works for Google) once wrote a blog post in which he claimed it was typical for junior faculty to travel twelve to twenty-four times a year. (Imagine the shallow efforts Nagpal avoided in sidestepping an extra ten to fifteen trips!) The travel quota is just one of several tactics that Nagpal used to control her workday (she also, for example, placed limits on the number of papers she would review per year), but what all her tactics shared was a commitment to ruthlessly capping the shallow while protecting the deep efforts—that is, original research—that ultimately determined her professional fate.

Returning to my own example, it's a similar commitment that enables me to succeed with fixed scheduling. I, too, am incredibly cautious about my use of the most dangerous word in one's productivity vocabulary: "yes." It takes a lot to convince me to agree to something that yields shallow work. If you ask for my involvement in university business that's not absolutely necessary, I might respond with a defense I learned from the department chair who hired me: "Talk to me after tenure." Another tactic that works well for me is to be clear in my refusal but ambiguous in my explanation for the refusal. The key is to avoid providing enough specificity about the excuse that the requester has the opportunity to defuse it. If, for example, I turn down a time-consuming speaking invitation with the excuse that I have other trips scheduled for around the same time, I don't provide details—which might leave the requester the ability to suggest a way to fit his or her event into my existing obligations—but instead just say, "Sounds interesting, but

I can't make it due to schedule conflicts." In turning down obligations, I also resist the urge to offer a consolation prize that ends up devouring almost as much of my schedule (e.g., "Sorry I can't join your committee, but I'm happy to take a look at some of your proposals as they come together and offer my thoughts"). A clean break is best.

In addition to carefully guarding my obligations, I'm incredibly conscientious about managing my time. Because my time is limited each day, I cannot afford to allow a large deadline to creep up on me, or a morning to be wasted on something trivial, because I didn't take a moment to craft a smart plan. The Damoclean cap on the workday enforced by fixed-schedule productivity has a way of keeping my organization efforts sharp. Without this looming cutoff, I'd likely end up more lax in my habits.

To summarize these observations, Nagpal and I can both succeed in academia without Tom-style overload due to two reasons. First, we're asymmetric in the culling forced by our fixed-schedule commitment. By ruthlessly reducing the shallow while preserving the deep, this strategy frees up our time without diminishing the amount of new value we generate. Indeed, I would go so far as to argue that the reduction in shallow frees up *more* energy for the deep alternative, allowing us to produce more than if we had defaulted to a more typical crowded schedule. Second, the limits to our time necessitate more careful thinking about our organizational habits, also leading to more value produced as compared to longer but less organized schedules.

The key claim of this strategy is that these same benefits

hold for most knowledge work fields. That is, even if you're not a professor, fixed-schedule productivity can yield powerful benefits. In most knowledge work jobs, it can be difficult in the moment to turn down a shallow commitment that seems harmless in isolation—be it accepting an invitation to get coffee or agreeing to "jump on a call." A commitment to fixed-schedule productivity, however, shifts you into a scarcity mind-set. Suddenly any obligation beyond your deepest efforts is suspect and seen as potentially disruptive. Your default answer becomes no, the bar for gaining access to your time and attention rises precipitously, and you begin to organize the efforts that pass these obstacles with a ruthless efficiency. It might also lead you to test assumptions about your company's work culture that you thought were ironclad but turn out to be malleable. It's common, for example, to receive e-mails from your boss after hours. Fixed-schedule productivity would have you ignore these messages until the next morning. Many suspect that this would cause problems, as such responses are *expected*, but in many cases, the fact that your boss happens to be clearing her inbox at night doesn't mean that she expects an immediate response—a lesson this strategy would soon help you discover.

Fixed-schedule productivity, in other words, is a *meta-habit* that's simple to adopt but broad in its impact. If you have to choose just one behavior that reorients your focus toward the deep, this one should be high on your list of possibilities. If you're still not sure, however, about the idea that artificial limits on your workday can make you more successful, I urge you to once again turn your attention to the career of fixed-schedule advocate Radhika Nagpal. In a satisfying coincidence, at almost the exact same time that Tom was lamenting online about his unavoidably intense workload as a young professor, Nagpal was celebrating the latest of the many professional triumphs she has experienced despite her fixed schedule: Her research was featured on the cover of the journal *Science*.

Become Hard to Reach

No discussion of shallow work is complete without considering e-mail. This quintessential shallow activity is particularly insidious in its grip on most knowledge workers' attention, as it delivers a steady stream of distractions *addressed specifically to you*. Ubiquitous e-mail access has become so ingrained in our professional habits that we're beginning to lose the sense that we have any say in its role in our life. As John Freeman warns in his 2009 book, *The Tyranny of E-mail*, with the rise of this technology "we are slowly eroding our ability to explain—in a careful, complex way—why it is so wrong for us to complain, resist, or redesign our workdays so that they are manageable." E-mail seems a fait accompli. Resistance is futile.

This strategy pushes back at this fatalism. Just because you cannot avoid this tool altogether doesn't mean you have to cede all authority over its role in your mental landscape. In the following sections I describe three tips that will help you regain authority over how this technology accesses your time and attention, and arrest the erosion of autonomy identified by Freeman. Resistance is not futile: You have more control over your electronic communication than you might at first assume.

Tip #1: Make People Who Send You E-mail Do More Work

Most nonfiction authors are easy to reach. They include an e-mail address on their author websites along with an open invitation to send them any request or suggestion that comes to mind. Many even encourage this feedback as a necessary commitment to the elusive but much-touted importance of "community building" among their readers. But here's the thing: *I don't buy it.*

If you visit the contact page on my author website, there's no general-purpose e-mail address. Instead, I list different individuals you can contact for specific purposes: my literary agent for rights requests, for example, or my speaking agent for speaking requests. If you want to reach me, I offer only a special-purpose e-mail address that comes with conditions and a lowered expectation that I'll respond:

> *If you have an offer, opportunity, or introduction that might make my life more interesting, e-mail me at* **interesting [at] calnewport.com**. *For the reasons stated above, I'll only respond to those proposals that are a good match for my schedule and interests.*

I call this approach a *sender filter*, as I'm asking my correspondents to filter themselves before attempting to contact me. This filter has significantly reduced the time I spend in my inbox. Before I began using a sender filter, I had a standard general-purpose e-mail address listed on my website. Not surprisingly, I used to receive a large volume of long e-mails asking for advice on specific (and often quite complicated) student or career questions. I like to help individuals, but these requests became overwhelming—they didn't take the senders long to craft but they would require a lot of explanation and writing on my part to respond. My sender filter has eliminated most such communication, and in doing so, has drastically reduced the number of messages I encounter in my writing inbox. As for my own interest in helping my readers, I now redirect this energy toward settings I carefully choose to maximize impact. Instead of allowing any student in the world to send me a question, for example, I now work closely with a small number of student groups where I'm quite accessible and can offer more substantial and effective mentoring.

Another benefit of a sender filter is that it resets expectations. The most crucial line in my description is the following: "I'll only respond to those proposals that are a good match for my schedule and interests." This seems minor, but it makes a substantial difference in how my correspondents think about their messages to me. The default social convention surrounding e-mail is that unless you're famous, if someone sends you something, you owe him or her a response. For most, therefore, an inbox full of messages generates a major sense of obligation.

By instead resetting your correspondents' expectations

to the reality that you'll probably *not* respond, the experience is transformed. The inbox is now a collection of opportunities that you can glance at when you have the free time—seeking out those that make sense for you to engage. But the pile of unread messages no longer generates a sense of obligation. You could, if you wanted to, ignore them all, and nothing bad would happen. Psychologically, this can be freeing.

I worried when I first began using a sender filter that it would seem pretentious—as if my time was more valuable than that of my readers—and that it would upset people. But this fear wasn't realized. Most people easily accept the idea that you have a right to control *your own* incoming communication, as they would like to enjoy this same right. More important, people appreciate clarity. Most are okay to not receive a response if they don't expect one (in general, those with a minor public presence, such as authors, overestimate how much people really care about their replies to their messages).

In some cases, this expectation reset might even earn you *more* credit when you do respond. For example, an editor of an online publication once sent me a guest post opportunity with the assumption, set by my filter, that I would likely not respond. When I did, it proved a happy surprise. Here's her summary of the interaction:

> *So, when I emailed Cal to ask if he wanted to contribute to [the publication], my expectations were set. He didn't have anything on his [sender filter] about wanting to guest blog, so there wouldn't have been any hard*

feelings if I'd never heard a peep. Then, when he did
respond, I was thrilled.

My particular sender filter is just one example of this
general strategy. Consider consultant Clay Herbert, who is
an expert in running crowd-funding campaigns for technology start-ups: a specialty that attracts a lot of correspondents hoping to glean some helpful advice. As a Forbes.com
article on sender filters reports, "At some point, the number of people reaching out exceeded [Herbert's] capacity, so
he created filters that put the onus on the person asking for
help."

Though he started from a similar motivation as me,
Herbert's filters ended up taking a different form. To contact him, you must first consult an FAQ to make sure your
question has not already been answered (which was the case
for a lot of the messages Herbert was processing before his
filters were in place). If you make it through this FAQ sieve,
he then asks you to fill out a survey that allows him to further screen for connections that seem particularly relevant to
his expertise. For those who make it past this step, Herbert
enforces a small fee you must pay before communicating
with him. This fee is not about making extra money, but is
instead about selecting for individuals who are serious about
receiving and acting on advice. Herbert's filters still enable
him to help people and encounter interesting opportunities.
But at the same time, they have reduced his incoming communication to a level he can easily handle.

To give another example, consider Antonio Centeno, who runs the popular *Real Man Style* blog. Centeno's sender filter lays out a two-step process. If you have a question, he diverts you to a public location to post it. Centeno thinks it's wasteful to answer the same questions again and again in private one-on-one conversations. If you make it past this step, he then makes you commit to, by clicking check boxes, the following three promises:

✓ I am not asking Antonio a style question I could find searching Google for 10 minutes.

✓ I am not SPAMMING Antonio with a cut-and-pasting generic request to promote my unrelated business.

✓ I will do a good deed for some random stranger if Antonio responds within 23 hours.

The message box in which you can type your message doesn't appear on the contact page until after you've clicked the box by all three promises.

To summarize, the technologies underlying e-mail are transformative, but the current social conventions guiding how we apply this technology are underdeveloped. The notion that all messages, regardless of purpose or sender, arrive in the same undifferentiated inbox, and that there's an expectation that every message deserves a (timely) response, is absurdly unproductive. The sender filter is a small but useful step toward a better state of affairs, and is an idea whose time has come—at least for the increasing number of entre-preneurs and freelancers who both receive a lot of incoming communication and have the ability to dictate their accessibility. (I'd also love to see similar rules become ubiquitous for intra-office communication in large organizations, but for the reasons argued in Chapter 2, we're probably a long way from that reality.) If you're in a position to do so, consider sender filters as a way of reclaiming some control over your time and attention.

Tip #2: Do More Work When You *Send or Reply to E-mails*

Consider the following standard e-mails:

E-mail #1: "It was great to meet you last week. I'd love to follow up on some of those issues we discussed. Do you want to grab coffee?"

E-mail #2: "We should get back to the research problem we discussed during my last visit. Remind me where we are with that?"

E-mail #3: "I took a stab at that article we discussed. It's attached. Thoughts?"

These three examples should be familiar to most knowledge workers, as they're representative of many of the messages that fill their inboxes. They're also potential productivity land mines: How you respond to them will have a significant impact on how much time and attention the resulting conversation ultimately consumes.

In particular, interrogative e-mails like these generate an initial instinct to dash off the quickest possible response that will clear the message—temporarily—out of your inbox. A quick response will, in the short term, provide you with some minor relief because you're bouncing the responsibility implied by the message off your court and back onto the sender's. This relief, however, is short-lived, as this responsibility will continue to bounce back again and again, continually sapping your time and attention. I suggest, therefore, that the right strategy when faced with a question of this type is to pause a moment before replying and take the time to answer the following key prompt:

> *What is the* project *represented by this message, and what is the most efficient (in terms of messages generated)* process *for bringing this project to a successful conclusion?*

Once you've answered this question for yourself, replace a quick response with one that takes the time to describe the process you identified, points out the current step, and emphasizes the step that comes next. I call this the *process-centric approach* to e-mail, and it's designed to minimize both the number of e-mails you receive and the amount of mental clutter they generate.

To better explain this process and why it works consider the following process-centric responses to the sample e-mails from earlier:

Process-Centric Response to E-mail #1: "I'd love to grab coffee. Let's meet at the Starbucks on campus. Below I listed two days next week when I'm free. For each day, I listed three times. If any of those day and time combinations work for you, let me know. I'll consider your reply confirmation for the meeting. If none of those date and time combinations work, give me a call at the number below and we'll hash out a time that works. Looking forward to it."

Process-Centric Response to E-mail #2: "I agree that we should return to this problem. Here's what I suggest...

"Sometime in the next week e-mail me everything you remember about our discussion on the problem. Once I receive that message, I'll start a shared directory for the project and add to it a document that summarizes what you sent me, combined with my own memory of our past discussion. In the document, I'll highlight the two or three most promising next steps.

"We can then take a crack at those next steps for a few weeks and check back in. I suggest we schedule a phone call for a month from now for this purpose. Below I listed some dates and times when I'm available for a call. When you respond with your notes, indicate the date and time combination that works best for you and we'll consider that reply confirmation for the call. I look forward to digging into this problem."

Process-Centric Response to E-mail #3: "Thanks for getting back to me. I'm going to read this draft of the article and send you back an edited version annotated with comments on Friday (the 10th). In this version I send back, I'll edit what I can do myself, and add comments to draw your attention to places where I think you're better suited to make the improvement. At that point, you should have what you need to polish and submit the final draft, so I'll leave you to do that—no need to reply to this message or to follow up with me after I return the edits—unless, of course, there's an issue."

In crafting these sample responses, I started by identifying the project implied by the message. Notice, the word "project" is used loosely here. It can cover things that are large and obviously projects, such as making progress on a research problem (Example #2), but it applies just as easily to small logistical challenges like setting up a coffee meeting (Example #1). I then took a minute or two to think through a process that gets us from the current state to a desired outcome with a minimum of messages required. The final step was to write a reply that clearly describes this process and where we stand. These examples centered on an e-mail reply, but it should be clear that a similar approach also works when writing an e-mail message from scratch.

The process-centric approach to e-mail can significantly mitigate the impact of this technology on your time and attention. There are two reasons for this effect. First, it reduces the number of e-mails in your inbox—sometimes significantly (something as simple as scheduling a coffee meeting can easily spiral into half a dozen or more messages over a period of many days, if you're not careful about your replies). This, in turn, reduces the time you spend in your inbox and reduces the brainpower you must expend when you do.

Second, to steal terminology from David Allen, a good process-centric message immediately "closes the loop" with respect to the project at hand. When a project is initiated by an e-mail that you send or receive, it squats in your mental landscape—becoming something that's "on your plate" in the sense that it has been brought to your attention and eventually needs to be addressed. This method closes this open loop as soon as it forms. By working through the whole process, adding to your task lists and calendar any relevant commitments on your part, and bringing the other party up to speed, your mind can reclaim the mental real estate the project once demanded. Less mental clutter means more mental resources available for deep thinking.

Process-centric e-mails might not seem natural at first. For one thing, they require that you spend more time thinking about your messages before you compose them. In the moment, this might seem like you're spending *more* time on e-mail. But the important point to remember is that the extra two to three minutes you spend at this point will save you many more minutes reading and responding to unnecessary extra messages later.

The other issue is that process-centric messages can seem stilted and overly technical. The current social conventions surrounding e-mail promote a conversational tone that clashes with the more systematic schedules or decision trees commonly used in process-centric communication. If this concerns you, I suggest that you add a longer conversational preamble to your messages. You can even separate the process-centric portion of the message from the conversational opening with a divider line, or label it "Proposed Next Steps," so that its technical tone seems more appropriate in context.

In the end, these minor hassles are worth it. By putting more thought up front into what's really being proposed by the e-mail messages that flit in and out of your inbox, you'll greatly reduce the negative impact of this technology on your ability to do work that actually matters.

Tip #3: Don't Respond

As a graduate student at MIT, I had the opportunity to interact with famous academics. In doing so, I noticed that many shared a fascinating and somewhat rare approach to e-mail: Their default behavior when receiving an e-mail message is to *not* respond.

Over time, I learned the philosophy driving this behavior: When it comes to e-mail, they believed, it's the sender's responsibility to convince the receiver that a reply is worthwhile. If you didn't make a convincing case *and* sufficiently minimize the effort required by the professor to respond, you didn't get a response.

For example, the following e-mail would likely not generate a reply with many of the famous names at the Institute:

> *Hi professor. I'd love to stop by sometime to talk about*
> *<topic X>. Are you available?*

Responding to this message requires too much work ("Are you available?" is too vague to be answered quickly). Also, there's no attempt to argue that this chat is worth the professor's time. With these critiques in mind, here's a version of the same message that would be more likely to generate a reply:

> *Hi professor. I'm working on a project similar to <topic*
> *X> with my advisor, <professor Y>. Is it okay if I stop*
> *by in the last fifteen minutes of your office hours on*
> *Thursday to explain what we're up to in more detail*
> *and see if it might complement your current project?*

Unlike the first message, this one makes a clear case for why this meeting makes sense and minimizes the effort needed from the receiver to respond.

This tip asks that you replicate, to the extent feasible in your professional context, this professorial ambivalence to e-mail. To help you in this effort, try applying the following three rules to sort through which messages require a response and which do not.

<u>Professorial E-mail Sorting</u>: Do not reply to an e-mail message if any of the following applies:

- It's ambiguous or otherwise makes it hard for you to generate a reasonable response.
- It's not a question or proposal that interests you.
- Nothing really good would happen if you did respond and nothing really bad would happen if you didn't.

In all cases, there are many obvious exceptions. If an ambiguous message about a project you don't care about comes from your company's CEO, for example, you'll respond. But looking beyond these exceptions, this professorial approach asks you to become way more ruthless when deciding whether or not to click "reply."

This tip can be uncomfortable at first because it will cause you to break a key convention currently surrounding e-mail: Replies are assumed, regardless of the relevance or appropriateness of the message. There's also no way to avoid that some bad things will happen if you take this approach. At the minimum, some people might get confused or upset—especially if they've never seen standard e-mail conventions questioned or ignored. Here's the thing: This is okay. As the author Tim Ferriss once wrote: "Develop the habit of letting small bad things happen. If you don't, you'll never find time for the life-changing big things." It should comfort you to realize that, as the professors at MIT discovered, people are quick to adjust their expectations to the specifics of your communication habits. The fact you didn't respond to their hastily scribed messages is probably not a central event in their lives.

Once you get past the discomfort of this approach, you'll begin to experience its rewards. There are two common tropes bandied around when people discuss solutions to e-mail overload. One says that sending e-mails generates more e-mails, while the other says that wrestling with ambiguous or irrelevant e-mails is a major source of inbox-related stress. The approach suggested here responds aggressively to both issues—you send fewer e-mails and ignore those that aren't easy to process—and by doing so will significantly weaken the grip your inbox maintains over your time and attention.

Conclusion

The story of Microsoft's founding has been told so many times that it's entered the realm of legend. In the winter of 1974, a young Harvard student named Bill Gates sees the Altair, the world's first personal computer, on the cover of *Popular Electronics*. Gates realizes that there's an opportunity to design software for the machine, so he drops everything and with the help of Paul Allen and Monte Davidoff spends the next eight weeks hacking together a version of the BASIC programming language for the Altair. This story is often cited as an example of Gates's insight and boldness, but recent interviews have revealed another trait that played a crucial role in the tale's happy ending: Gates's preternatural deep work ability.

As Walter Isaacson explained in a 2013 article on the topic for the *Harvard Gazette*, Gates worked with such intensity for such lengths during this two-month stretch that he would often collapse into sleep on his keyboard in the middle of writing a line of code. He would then sleep for an hour or two, wake up, and pick up right where he left off—an ability that a still-impressed Paul Allen describes as "a prodigious feat of concentration." In his book *The Innovators*, Isaacson later summarized Gates's unique tendency toward depth as follows: "The one trait that differentiated [Gates from Allen] was focus. Allen's mind would flit between many ideas and passions, but Gates was a serial obsessor."

It's here, in this story of Gates's obsessive focus, that we encounter the strongest form of my argument for deep work. It's easy, amid the turbulence of a rapidly evolving information age, to default to dialectical grumbling. The curmudgeons among us are vaguely uneasy about the attention people pay to their phones, and pine for the days of unhurried concentration, while the digital hipsters equate such nostalgia with Luddism and boredom, and believe that increased connection is the foundation for a utopian future. Marshall McLuhan declared that "the medium is the message," but our current conversation on these topics seems to imply that "the medium is morality"—either you're on board with the Facebook future or see it as our downfall.

As I emphasized in this book's introduction, I have no interest in this debate. A commitment to deep work is not a moral stance and it's not a philosophical statement—it is instead a pragmatic recognition that the ability to concentrate is a skill that *gets valuable things done*. Deep work is important, in other words, not because distraction is evil, but because it enabled Bill Gates to start a billion-dollar industry in less than a semester.

This is also a lesson, as it turns out, that I've personally relearned again and again in my own career. I've been a depth devotee for more than a decade, but even I am still regularly surprised by its power. When I was in graduate school, the period when I first encountered and started prioritizing this skill, I found that deep work allowed me to write a pair of quality peer-reviewed papers each year (a respectable rate for a student), while rarely having to work past five on weekdays or work at all on weekends (a rarity among my peers).

As I neared my transition to professorship, however, I began to worry. As a student and a postdoc my time commitments were minimal—leaving me most of my day to shape as I desired. I knew I would lose this luxury in the next phase of my career, and I wasn't confident in my ability to integrate enough deep work into this more demanding schedule to maintain my productivity. Instead of just stewing in my anxiety, I decided to do something about it: I created a plan to bolster my deep work muscles.

These training efforts were deployed during my last two years at MIT, while I was a postdoc starting to look for professor positions. My main tactic was to introduce artificial constraints on my schedule, so as to better approximate the more limited free time I expected as a professor. In addition to my rule about not working at night, I started to take extended lunch breaks in the middle of the day to go for a run and then eat lunch back at my apartment. I also signed a deal to write my fourth book, *So Good They Can't Ignore You*, during this period—a project, of course, that soon levied its own intense demands on my time.

To compensate for these new constraints, I refined my ability to work deeply. Among other methods, I began to more carefully block out deep work hours and preserve them against incursion. I also developed an ability to carefully work through thoughts during the many hours I spent on foot each week (a boon to my productivity), and became obsessive about finding disconnected locations conducive to focus. During the summer, for example, I would often work under the dome in Barker Engineering library—a pleasingly cavernous location that becomes too crowded when class is in session, and during the winter, I sought more obscure locations for some silence, eventually developing a preference for the small but well-appointed Lewis Music Library. At some point, I even bought a $50 high-end grid-lined lab notebook to work on mathematical proofs, believing that its expense would induce more care in my thinking.

I ended up surprised by how well this recommitment to depth ended up working. After I'd taken a job as a computer science professor at Georgetown University in the fall of 2011, my obligations did in fact drastically increase. But I had been training for this moment. Not only did I preserve my research productivity; it actually *improved*. My previous rate of two good papers a year, which I maintained as an unencumbered graduate student, leapt to four good papers a year, on average, once I became a much more encumbered professor.

Impressive as this was to me, however, I was soon to learn that I had not yet reached the limits of what deep work could produce. This lesson would come during my third year as a professor. During my third year at Georgetown, which spanned the fall of 2013 through the summer of

2014, I turned my attention back to my deep work habits, searching for more opportunities to improve. A big reason for this recommitment to depth is the book you're currently reading—most of which was written during this period. Writing a seventy-thousand-word book manuscript, of course, placed a sudden new constraint on my already busy schedule, and I wanted to make sure my academic productivity didn't take a corresponding hit. Another reason I turned back to depth was the looming tenure process. I had a year or two of publications left before my tenure case was submitted. *This* was the time, in other words, to make a statement about my abilities (especially given that my wife and I were planning on growing our family with a second child in the final year before tenure). The final reason I turned back to depth was more personal and (admittedly) a touch petulant. I had applied and been rejected for a well-respected grant that many of my colleagues were receiving. I was upset and embarrassed, so I decided that instead of just complaining or wallowing in self-doubt, I would compensate for losing the grant by increasing the rate and impressiveness of my publications—allowing them to declare on my behalf that I actually *did* know what I was doing, even if this one particular grant application didn't go my way.

I was already an adept deep worker, but these three forces drove me to push this habit to an extreme. I became ruthless in turning down time-consuming commitments and began to work more in isolated locations outside my office. I placed a tally of my deep work hours in a prominent position near my desk and got upset when it failed to grow at a fast enough rate. Perhaps most impactful, I returned to my MIT habit of working on problems in my head whenever a good time presented itself—be it walking the dog or commuting. Whereas earlier, I tended to increase my deep work only as a deadline approached, this year I was relentless—most every day of most every week I was pushing my mind to grapple with results of consequence, regardless of whether or not a specific deadline was near. I solved proofs on subway rides and while shoveling snow. When my son napped on the weekend, I would pace the yard thinking, and when stuck in traffic I would methodically work through problems that were stymieing me.

As this year progressed, I became a deep work machine—and the result of this transformation caught me off guard. During the same year that I wrote a book and my oldest son entered the terrible twos, I managed to more than double my average academic productivity, publishing *nine* peer-reviewed papers—all the while maintaining my prohibition on work in the evenings.

———

I'm the first to admit that my year of extreme depth was perhaps a bit too extreme: It proved cognitively exhausting, and going forward I'll likely moderate this intensity. But this experience reinforces the point that opened this conclusion: Deep work is *way more* powerful than most people understand. It's a commitment to this skill that allowed Bill Gates to make the most of an unexpected opportunity to create a new industry, and that allowed me to double my academic productivity the same year I decided to concurrently write a book. To leave the distracted masses to join the focused few, I'm arguing, is a transformative experience.

The deep life, of course, is not for everybody. It requires hard work and drastic changes to your habits. For many, there's a comfort in the artificial busyness of rapid e-mail messaging and social media posturing, while the deep life demands that you leave much of that behind. There's also an uneasiness that surrounds any effort to produce the best things you're capable of producing, as this forces you to confront the possibility that your best is not (yet) that good. It's safer to comment on our culture than to step into the Rooseveltian ring and attempt to wrestle it into something better.

But if you're willing to sidestep these comforts and fears, and instead struggle to deploy your mind to its fullest capacity to create things that matter, then you'll discover, as others have before you, that depth generates a life rich with productivity and meaning. In Part 1, I quoted writer Winifred Gallagher saying, "I'll live the focused life, because it's the best kind there is." I agree. So does Bill Gates. And hopefully now that you've finished this book, you agree too.

Notes

Introduction

"In my retiring room"; **"I keep the key"**; and **"The feeling of repose and renewal"**: Jung, Carl. *Memories, Dreams, Reflections.* Trans. Richard Winston. New York: Pantheon, 1963.

"Although he had many patients" and other information on artists' habits: Currey, Mason. *Daily Rituals: How Artists Work.* New York: Knopf, 2013.

The following timeline of Jung's life and work also proved useful in untangling the role of deep work in his career: Cowgill, Charles. "Carl Jung." May 1997. http://www.muskingum.edu/~psych/ psycweb/history/jung.htm.

Anders Ericsson from Florida State University is a leading academic researcher on the concept of deliberate practice. He has a nice description of the idea on his academic website: http://www.psy .fsu.edu/faculty/ericsson/ericsson.exp.perf.html.

My list of the deep work habits of important personalities draws from the following sources:

- Montaigne information comes from: Bakewell, Sarah. *How to Live: Or A Life of Montaigne in One Question and Twenty Attempts at an Answer.* New York: Other Press, 2010.
- Mark Twain information comes from: Mason Currey's *Daily Rituals.*
- Woody Allen information comes from Robert Weide's 2011 documentary, *Woody Allen: A Documentary.*

- Peter Higgs information comes from: Sample, Ian. "Peter Higgs Proves as Elusive as Higgs Boson after Nobel Success." *Guardian*, October 9, 2013, http://www.theguardian.com/science/2013/oct/08/nobel-laureate-peter-higgs-boson-elusive.
- J.K. Rowling information comes from: https://twitter.com/jk_rowling.
- Bill Gates information comes from: Guth, Robert. "In Secret Hideaway, Bill Gates Ponders Microsoft's Future." *Wall Street Journal*, March 28, 2005, http://online.wsj.com/news/articles/SB111196625830690477.
- Neal Stephenson information comes from an older version of Stephenson's website, which has been preserved in a December 2003 snapshot by The Internet Archive: http://web.archive.org/web/20031207060405/http://www.well.com/~neal/badcorrespondent.html.

"A 2012 McKinsey study found that": Chui, Michael, et al. "The Social Economy: Unlocking Value and Productivity Through Social Technologies." McKinsey Global Institute. July 2012. http://www.mckinsey.com/insights/high_tech_telecoms_internet/the_social_economy.

"What the Net seems to be doing is" and **"I'm not the only one"**: Carr, Nicholas. "Is Google Making Us Stupid?" *The Atlantic Monthly*, July–August 2008. http://www.theatlantic.com/magazine/archive/2008/07/is-google-making-us-stupid/306868/.

The fact that Carr had to move to a cabin to finish writing *The Shallows* comes from the Author's Note in the paperback version of the book.

"superpower of the 21st century": Barker, Eric. "Stay Focused: 5 Ways to Increase Your Attention Span." *Barking Up the Wrong Tree*. September 18, 2013. http://www.bakadesuyo.com/2013/09/stay-focused/.

Chapter 1

Information about Nate Silver's election traffic on the *New York Times* website: Tracy, Marc. "Nate Silver Is a One-Man Traffic Machine for the Times." *New Republic*, November 6, 2012. http://www.newrepublic.com/article/109714/nate-silvers-fivethirtyeight-blog-drawing-massive-traffic-new-york-times.

Information about Nate Silver's ESPN/ABC News deal: Allen, Mike. "How ESPN and ABC Landed Nate Silver." Politico, July 22, 2013. http://www.politico.com/blogs/media/2013/07/how-espn-and -abc-landed-nate-silver-168888.html.

Examples of concerns regarding Silver's methodology:

Davis, Sean M. "Is Nate Silver's Value at Risk?" Daily Caller, November 1, 2012. http://dailycaller.com/2012/11/01/is-nate-silvers-value -at-risk/.

Marcus, Gary, and Ernest Davis. "What Nate Silver Gets Wrong." *The New Yorker*, January 25, 2013. http://www.newyorker.com/online/ blogs/books/2013/01/what-nate-silver-gets-wrong.html.

Information about David Heinemeier Hansson comes from the following websites:

- David Heinemeier Hanson. http://david.heinemeierhansson.com/.
- Lindberg, Oliver. "The Secrets Behind 37signals' Success." TechRadar, September 6, 2010. http://www.techradar.com/us/ news/internet/the-secrets-behind-37signals-success-712499.
- "OAK Racing." Wikipedia. http://en.wikipedia.org/wiki/OAK _Racing.

For more on John Doerr's deals: "John Doerr." Forbes. http://www .forbes.com/profile/john-doerr/.

The $3.3 billion net worth of John Doerr was retrieved from the following Forbes.com profile page on April 10, 2014: http://www .forbes.com/profile/john-doerr/.

"We are in the early throes of a Great Restructuring" and **"Our technologies are racing ahead"**: from page 9 of Brynjolfsson, Erik, and Andrew McAfee. *Race Against the Machine: How the Digital Revolution Is Accelerating Innovation, Driving Productivity, and Irreversibly Transforming Employment and the Economy.* Cambridge, MA: Digital Frontier Press, 2011.

"other technologies like data visualization, analytics, high speed communications": Ibid., 9.

"The key question will be: are you good at working with intelligent machines or not?": from page 1 of Cowen, Tyler. *Average Is Over.* New York: Penguin, 2013.

Rosen, Sherwin. "The Economics of Superstars." *The American Economic Review* 71.5 (December 1981): 845–858.

"Hearing a succession of mediocre singers does not add up to a single outstanding performance": Ibid., 846.

The Instagram example and its significance for labor disparities were first brought to my attention by the writing/speaking of Jaron Lanier.

How to Become a Winner in the New Economy

Details on Nate Silver's tools:

- Hickey, Walter. "How to Become Nate Silver in 9 Simple Steps." *Business Insider*, November 14, 2012. http://www.business insider.com/how-nate-silver-and-fivethityeight-works-2012-11.
- Silver, Nate. "IAmA Blogger for FiveThirtyEight at The New York Times. Ask Me Anything." Reddit. http://www.reddit.com/r/ IAmA/comments/166yeo/iama_blogger_for_fivethirtyeight_at _the_new_york.
- "Why Use Stata." www.stata.com/why-use-stata/.

The SQL example I gave was from postgreSQL, an open source database system popular in both industry and (especially) academia. I don't know what specific system Silver uses, but it almost certainly requires some variant of the SQL language used in this example.

Deep Work Helps You Quickly Learn Hard Things

"Let your mind become a lens": from page 95 of Sertillanges, Antonin-Dalmace. *The Intellectual Life: Its Spirits, Conditions, Methods*. Trans. Mary Ryan. Cork, Ireland: Mercier Press, 1948.

"the development and deepening of the mind": Ibid., 13.

Details about deliberate practice draw heavily on the following seminal survey paper on the topic: Ericsson, K.A., R.T. Krampe, and C. Tesch-Römer. "The Role of Deliberate Practice in the Acquisition of Expert Performance." *Psychological Review* 100.3 (1993): 363–406.

"We deny that these differences [between expert performers and normal adults] are immutable": Ibid., 13.

"Men of genius themselves": from page 95 of Sertillanges, *The Intellectual Life*.

"Diffused attention is almost antithetical to the *focused attention* required by deliberate practice": from page 368 of Ericsson, Krampe, and Tesch-Romer. "The Role of Deliberate Practice in the Acquisition of Expert Performance."

Details on the neurobiology of expert performance can be found in: Coyle, *The Talent Code*.

Coyle also has a nice slideshow about myelination at his website: "Want to Be a Superstar Athlete? Build More Myelin." The Talent Code. www.thetalentcode.com/myelin.

For more on deliberate practice, the following two books provide a good popular overview:

- Colvin, Geoffrey. *Talent Is Overrated: What Really Separates World-Class Performers from Everybody Else*. New York: Portfolio, 2008.
- Coyle, Daniel. *The Talent Code: Greatness Isn't Born. It's Grown. Here's How*. New York: Bantam, 2009.

Deep Work Helps You Produce at an Elite Level

More about Adam Grant, his records, and his (thirty-page) CV can be found at his academic website: https://mgmt.wharton.upenn.edu/profile/1323/.

Grant, Adam. *Give and Take: Why Helping Others Drives Our Success*. New York: Viking Adult, 2013.

The article on Adam Grant in the *New York Times Magazine*: Dominus, Susan. "The Saintly Way to Succeed." *New York Times Magazine*, March 31, 2013: MM20.

Newport, Cal. *How to Become a Straight-A Student: The Unconventional Strategies Used by Real College Students to Score High While Studying Less*. New York: Three Rivers Press, 2006.

Leroy, Sophie. "Why Is It So Hard to Do My Work? The Challenge of Attention Residue When Switching Between Work Tasks." *Organizational Behavior and Human Decision Processes* 109 (2009): 168–181.

What About Jack Dorsey?

"He is a disrupter on a massive scale and a repeat offender" and **"I do a lot of my work at stand-up tables"** and details on Jack Dorsey's daily schedule come from the following Forbes.com article: Savitz, Eric. "Jack Dorsey: Leadership Secrets of Twitter and Square." Forbes, October 17, 2012. http://www.forbes.com/sites/ericsavitz/2012/10/17/jack-dorsey-the-leadership-secrets-of-twitter-and-square/3/.

The cited Jack Dorsey net worth number was accessed on the following Forbes.com profile on April 10, 2014: http://www.forbes.com/profile/jack-dorsey/.

"I can go a good solid Saturday without": from an interview with Kerry Trainor that was conducted in October 2013 by HuffPost Live. A clip with the e-mail usage quote is available here: http://www.kirotv.com/videos/technology/how-long-can-vimeo-ceo-kerry-trainor-go-without/vCCBLd/.

Chapter 2

"the largest open floor plan in the world" and other information about Facebook's new headquarters: Hoare, Rose. "Do Open Plan Offices Lead to Better Work or Closed Minds?" CNN, October 4, 2012. http://edition.cnn.com/2012/10/04/business/global-office-open-plan/.

"We encourage people to stay out in the open" and other information about Square's headquarters:

Savitz, Eric. "Jack Dorsey: Leadership Secrets of Twitter and Square." Forbes, October 17, 2012. http://www.forbes.com/sites/ericsavitz/2012/10/17/jack-dorsey-the-leadership-secrets-of-twitter-and-square.

"province of chatty teenagers" and **"new productivity gains"** from the following *New York Times* article about instant messaging: Strom, David. "I.M. Generation Is Changing the Way Business Talks." *New York Times*, April 5, 2006. http://www.nytimes.com/2006/04/05/technology/techspecial4/05message.html.

More on Hall can be found at Hall.com and in this article: Tsotsis, Alexia. "Hall.com Raises $580K from Founder's Collective and Others to Transform Realtime Collaboration." TechCrunch, October 16, 2011. http://techcrunch.com/2011/10/16/hall-com-raises-580k-from-founders-collective-and-others-to-transform-realtime-collaboration/.

An up-to-date list of the more than eight hundred *New York Times* employees using Twitter: https://twitter.com/nytimes/nyt-journalists/members.

The original Jonathan Franzen piece for the *Guardian* was published online on September 13, 2013, with the title "Jonathan Franzen: What's Wrong with the Modern World." The piece has since been removed for "legal" issues.

Here is the October 4, 2013, *Slate* piece, by Katy Waldman, that ended up titled "Jonathan Franzen's Lonely War on the Internet Continues." Notice from the URL that the original title was even harsher: http://www.slate.com/blogs/future_tense/2013/10/04/jonathan_franzen_says_twitter_is_a_coercive_development_is_grumpy_and_out.html.

"Franzen's a category of one": from Jennifer Weiner's response to Franzen in *The New Republic*: Weiner, Jennifer. "What Jonathan Franzen Misunderstands About Me." *New Republic*, September 18, 2013, http://www.newrepublic.com/article/114762/jennifer-weiner-responds-jonathan-franzen.

"massive distraction" and **"If you are just getting into some work"**: Treasure, Julian. "Sound News: More Damaging Evidence on Open Plan Offices." Sound Agency, November 16, 2011. http://www.thesoundagency.com/2011/sound-news/more-damaging-evidence-on-open-plan-offices/.

"This was reported by subjects" and related results from: Mark, Gloria, Victor M. Gonzalez, and Justin Harris. "No Task Left Behind? Examining the Nature of Fragmented Work." *Proceedings of the SIGCHI Conference on Human Factors in Computing Systems*. New York: ACM, 2005.

"Twitter is crack for media addicts" and other details of George Packer's thoughts about social media: Packer, George. "Stop the World." *The New Yorker*, January 29, 2010, http://www.newyorker.com/online/blogs/georgepacker/2010/01/stop-the-world.html.

The Metric Black Hole

"A 'free and frictionless' method of communication" and other details of Tom Cochran's e-mail experiment: Cochran, Tom. "Email Is Not Free." *Harvard Business Review*, April 8, 2013. http://blogs.hbr.org/2013/04/email-is-not-free/.

"it is objectively difficult to measure individual": from page 509 of Piketty, Thomas. *Capital in the Twenty-First Century*. Cambridge, MA: Belknap Press, 2014.

"undoubtedly true": Manzi, Jim. "Piketty's Can Opener." *National Review*, July 7, 2014. http://www.nationalreview.com/corner/382084/pikettys-can-opener-jim-manzi. This careful and critical review of Piketty's book by Jim Manzi is where I originally came across the Piketty citation.

The Principle of Least Resistance

"At first, the team resisted"; **"putting their careers in jeopardy"**; and **"a better product delivered to the client"** as well as a good summary of Leslie Perlow's connectivity research can be found in Perlow, Leslie A., and Jessica L. Porter. "Making Time Off Predictable—and Required." *Harvard Business Review*, October 2009. https://hbr.org/2009/10/making-time-off-predictable-and-required.

For more on David Allen's task management system, see his book: Allen, David. *Getting Things Done.* New York: Viking, 2001.

Allen's *fifteen-element* task management flowchart can be found in Allen, *Getting Things Done*, as well as online: http://gettingthingsdone.com/pdfs/tt_workflow_chart.pdf.

Busyness as a Proxy for Productivity

The h-index for an academic is (roughly speaking) the largest value x that satisfies the following rule: "I have published at least x papers with x or more citations." Notice, this value manages to capture both how many papers you have written and how often you are cited. You cannot gain a high h-index value simply by pumping out a lot of low-value papers, *or* by having a small number of papers that are cited often. This metric tends to grow over careers, which is why in many fields h-index goals are tied to certain career milestones.

"To do real good physics work": comes around the 28:20 mark in a 1981 TV interview with Richard Feynman for the BBC *Horizon* program (the interview aired in the United States as an episode of *NOVA*). The YouTube video of this interview that I watched when researching this book has since been removed due to a copyright complaint by the BBC (https://www.youtube.com/watch?v=Bgaw9qe7DEE). Transcripts of the relevant quote, however, can be found at http://articles.latimes.com/1988-02-16/news/mn-42968_1_nobel-prize/2 and http://calnewport.com/blog/2014/04/20/richard-feynman-didnt-win-a-nobel-by-responding-promptly-to-e-mails/ and http://www.worldcat.org/wcpa/servlet/DCARead?standardNo=0738201081&standardNoType=1&excerpt=true.

"Managers themselves inhabit a bewildering psychic landscape": from page 9 of Crawford, Matthew. *Shop Class as Soulcraft.* New York: Penguin, 2009.

"cranking widgets": This concept is a popular metaphor in discussing David Allen's task management system; c.f. Mann, Merlin. "Podcast: Interview with GTD's David Allen on Procrastination." 43 Folders, August 19, 2007. http://www.43folders.com/2006/10/10/productive-talk-procrastination; Schuller, Wayne. "The Power of Cranking Widgets." *Wayne Schuller's Blog*, April 9, 2008. http://schuller.id.au/2008/04/09/the-power-of-cranking-widgets-gtd-times/; and Babauta, Leo. "Cranking Widgets: Turn Your Work into Stress-free Productivity." Zen Habits, March 6, 2007. http://zenhabits.net/cranking-widgets-turn-your-work-into/.

More on Marissa Mayer's working-from-home prohibition: Carlson, Nicholas. "How Marissa Mayer Figured Out Work-At-Home Yahoos Were Slacking Off." Business Insider, March 2, 2013. http://www.businessinsider.com/how-marissa-mayer-figured-out-work-at-home-yahoos-were-slacking-off-2013-3.

The Cult of the Internet

Alissa Rubin tweets at @Alissanyt. I don't have specific evidence that Alissa Rubin was pressured to tweet. But I can make a circumstantial case: She includes "nyt" in her Twitter handle, and the *Times* maintains a social media desk that helps educate its employees about how to use social media (c.f. https://www.mediabistro.com/alltwitter/new-york-times-social-media-desk_b53783), a focus that has led to more than eight hundred employees tweeting: https://twitter.com/nytimes/nyt-journalists/members.

Here is an example of one of Alissa Rubin's articles that I encountered when writing this chapter: Rubin, Alissa J., and Maïa de la Baume, "Claims of French Complicity in Rwanda's Genocide Rekindle Mutual Resentment." *New York Times*, April 8, 2014. http://www.nytimes.com/2014/04/09/world/africa/claims-of-french-complicity-in-rwandas-genocide-rekindle-mutual-resentment.html?ref=alissajohannsenrubin.

Postman, Neil. *Technopoly: The Surrender of Culture to Technology*. New York: Vintage Books, 1993.

"It does not make them illegal": Ibid., 48.

"It's this propensity to view 'the Internet' as a source of wisdom": from page 25 of Morozov, Evgeny. *To Save Everything, Click Here*. New York: Public Affairs, 2013.

Chapter 3

"I do all my work by hand": from Ric Furrer's artist statement, which can be found online, along with general biographical details on Furrer and information about his business: http://www.doorcounty forgeworks.com.

"This part, the initial breakdown"; **"You have to be very gentle"**; **"It's ready"**; and **"To do it right, it is the most complicated thing"**: from the PBS documentary "Secrets of the Viking Swords," which is an episode of *NOVA* that first aired on September 25, 2013. For more information on the episode and online streaming see: http:// www.pbs.org/wgbh/nova/ancient/secrets-viking-sword.html.

"The satisfactions of manifesting oneself concretely": from page 15 of Crawford, *Shop Class as Soulcraft*.

"The world of information superhighways": from Ric Furrer's artist statement: http://www.doorcountyforgeworks.com.

A Neurological Argument for Depth

"not just cancer"; **"This disease wanted to"**; and **"movies, walks"**: from page 3 of Gallagher, Winifred. *Rapt: Attention and the Focused Life*. New York, Penguin, 2009.

"Like fingers pointing to the moon": Ibid., 2.

"Who you are": Ibid., 1.

"reset button": Ibid., 48.

"Rather than continuing to focus": Ibid., 49.

Though *Rapt* provides a good summary of Barbara Fredrickson's research on positivity (see pages 48–49), more details can be found in Fredrickson's 2009 book on the topic: Frederickson, Barbara. *Positivity: Groundbreaking Research Reveals How to Embrace the Hidden Strength of Positive Emotions, Overcome Negativity, and Thrive*. New York: Crown Archetype, 2009.

The Laura Carstensen research was featured in *Rapt* (see pages 50–51). For more information, see the following article: Carstensen, Laura L., and Joseph A. Mikels. "At the Intersection of Emotion and Cognition: Aging and the Positivity Effect." *Current Directions in Psychological Science* 14.3 (2005): 117–121.

"concentration so intense": from page 71 of Csikszentmihalyi, Mihaly. *Flow: The Psychology of Optimal Experience*. New York: Harper & Row Publishers, 1990.

"Five years of reporting": from page 13 of Gallagher, *Rapt.*
"I'll choose my targets with care": Ibid., 14.

A Psychological Argument for Depth

For more on the experience sampling method, read the original article here:
Larson, Reed, and Mihaly Csikszentmihalyi. "The Experience Sampling Method." *New Directions for Methodology of Social & Behavioral Science.* 15 (1983): 41-56.
You can also find a short summary of the technique at Wikipedia: http://en.wikipedia.org/wiki/Experience_sampling_method.
"The best moments usually occur": from page 3 of Csikszentmihalyi, *Flow.*
"Ironically, jobs are actually easier to enjoy": Ibid., 162.
"jobs should be redesigned": Ibid., 157.

A Philosophical Argument for Depth

"The world used to be": from page xi of Dreyfus, Hubert, and Sean Dorrance Kelly. *All Things Shining: Reading the Western Classics to Find Meaning in a Secular Age.* New York: Free Press, 2011.
"The Enlightenment's metaphysical embrace": Ibid., 204.
"Because each piece of wood is distinct": Ibid., 210.
"is not to *generate* meaning": Ibid., 209.
"Beautiful code is short and concise": from a THNKR interview with Santiago Gonzalez available online: https://www.youtube.com/watch?v=DBXZWB_dNsw.
"We who cut mere stones" and **"Within the overall structure"**: from the preface of Hunt, Andrew, and David Thomas. *The Pragmatic Programmer: From Journeyman to Master.* New York: Addison-Wesley Professional, 1999.

Homo Sapiens Deepensis

"I'll live the focused life": from page 14 of Gallagher, *Rapt.*

Rule #1

Hofmann, W., R. Baumeister, G. Förster, and K. Vohs. "Everyday Temptations: An Experience Sampling Study of Desire, Conflict, and Self-Control." *Journal of Personality and Social Psychology* 102.6 (2012): 1318–1335.

"Desire turned out to be the norm, not the exception": from page 3 of Baumeister, Roy F., and John Tierney. *Willpower: Rediscovering the Greatest Human Strength*. New York: Penguin Press, 2011.

"taking a break from [hard] work": Ibid., 4.

Original study: Baumeister, R., E. Bratlavsky, M. Muraven, and D. M. Tice. "Ego Depletion: Is the Active Self a Limited Resource?" *Journal of Personality and Social Psychology* 74 (1998): 1252–1265.

Decide on Your Depth Philosophy

"What I do takes long hours of studying" and **"I have been a happy man"**: from Donald Knuth's Web page: http://www-cs-faculty .stanford.edu/~uno/email.html.

"Persons who wish to interfere with my concentration": from Neal Stephenson's old website, in a page titled "My Ongoing Battle with Continuous Partial Attention," archived in December 2003: http://web.archive.org/web/20031231203738/http://www.well .com/~neal/.

"The productivity equation is a non-linear one": from Neal Stephenson's old website, in a page titled "Why I Am a Bad Correspondent," archived in December 2003: http://web.archive.org/web/ 20031207060405/http://www.well.com/~neal/badcorrespondent .html.

Stephenson, Neal. *Anathem*. New York: William Morrow, 2008.

For more on the connection between *Anathem* and the tension between focus and distraction, see "Interview with Neal Stephenson," published on GoodReads.com in September 2008: http://www.good reads.com/interviews/show/14.Neal_Stephenson.

"I saw my chance": from the (Internet) famous "Don't Break the Chain" article by Brad Isaac, writing for Lifehacker.com: http:// lifehacker.com/281626/jerry-seinfelds-productivity-secret.

"one of the best magazine journalists": Hitchens, Christopher, "Touch of Evil." *London Review of Books*, October 22, 1992. http:// www.lrb.co.uk/v14/n20/christopher-hitchens/touch-of-evil.

Isaacson, Walter, and Evan Thomas. *The Wise Men: Six Friends and the World They Made*. New York: Simon and Schuster Reissue Edition, 2012. (The original version of this book was published in 1986, but it was recently republished in hardcover due presumably to Isaacson's recent publishing success.)

"richly textured account" and **"fashioned a Cold War Plutarch"**: from the excerpts of reviews of Walter Isaacson's *The Wise Men* that I found in the book jacket blurbs reproduced on Simon and Schuster's official website for the book: http://books.simonand schuster.com/The-Wise-Men/Walter-Isaacson/9781476728827.

Ritualize

"every inch of [Caro's] New York office" and **"I trained myself"** and other details about Robert Caro's habits: Darman, Jonathan. "The Marathon Man," *Newsweek*, February 16, 2009, which I discovered through the following post, "Robert Caro," on Mason Currey's *Daily Routines* blog: http://dailyroutines.typepad.com/daily_routines/2009/02/robert-caro.html.

The Charles Darwin information was brought to my attention by the "Charles Darwin" post on Mason Currey's *Daily Routines*, December 11, 2008. http://dailyroutines.typepad.com/daily_routines/2008/12/charles-darwin.html.

This post, in turn, draws on *Charles Darwin: A Companion* by R.B. Freeman, accessed by Currey on The Complete Work of Charles Darwin Online.

"There is a popular notion that artists": from the following Slate .com article: Currey, Mason. "Daily Rituals." *Slate*, May 16, 2013. http://www.slate.com/articles/arts/culturebox/features/2013/daily_rituals/john_updike_william_faulkner_chuck_close_they _didn_t_wait_for_inspiration.html.

"[Great creative minds] think like artists": from Brooks, David. "The Good Order." *New York Times*, September 25, 2014, op-ed. http://www.nytimes.com/2014/09/26/opinion/david-brooks -routine-creativity-and-president-obamas-un-speech.html?_r=1.

"It is only ideas gained from walking that have any worth": This Nietzsche quote was brought to my attention by the excellent book on walking and philosophy: Gros, Frédérick. *A Philosophy of Walking*. Trans. John Howe. New York: Verso Books, 2014.

Make Grand Gestures

"As I was finishing *Deathly Hallows* there came a day": from the transcript of Rowling's 2010 interview with Oprah Winfrey on

Harry Potter's Page: http://www.harrypotterspage.com/2010/10/03/transcript-of-oprah-interview-with-j-k-rowling/.

Details regarding J.K. Rowling working at the Balmoral Hotel: Johnson, Simon. "Harry Potter Fans Pay £1,000 a Night to Stay in Hotel Room Where JK Rowling Finished Series." *Telegraph*, July 20, 2008. http://www.telegraph.co.uk/news/celebritynews/2437835/Harry-Potter-fans-pay-1000-a-night-to-stay-in-hotel-room-where-JK-Rowling-finished-series.html.

For more on Bill Gates's Think Weeks: Guth, Robert A. "In Secret Hideaway, Bill Gates Ponders Microsoft's Future." *Wall Street Journal*, March 28, 2005. http://online.wsj.com/news/articles/SB111196625830690477?mg=reno64-wsj.

"It's really about two and a half months": from the following author interview: Birnbaum, Robert. "Alan Lightman." Identity Theory, November 16, 2000. http://www.identitytheory.com/alan-lightman/.

Michael Pollan's book about building a writing cabin: Pollan, Michael. *A Place of My Own: The Education of an Amateur Builder*. New York: Random House, 1997.

For more on William Shockley's scramble to invent the junction transistor: "Shockley Invents the Junction Transistor." PBS. http://www.pbs.org/transistor/background1/events/junctinv.html.

"'Ohh! Shiny!' DNA": from a blog post by Shankman: "Where's Your Home?" Peter Shankman's website, July 2, 2014, http://shankman.com/where-s-your-home/.

"The trip cost $4,000": from an interview with Shankman: Machan, Dyan. "Why Some Entrepreneurs Call ADHD a Superpower." MarketWatch, July 12, 2011. http://www.marketwatch.com/story/entrepreneurs-superpower-for-some-its-adhd-1310052627559.

Don't Work Alone

The July 2013 *Bloomberg Businessweek* article by Venessa Wong titled "Ending the Tyranny of the Open-Plan Office": http://www.bloomberg.com/articles/2013-07-01/ending-the-tyranny-of-the-open-plan-office. This article has more background on the damage of open office spaces on worker productivity.

The twenty-eight hundred workers cited in regard to Facebook's open office size was taken from the following March 2014 *Daily Mail* article: Prigg, Mark. "Now That's an Open Plan Office." http://

www.dailymail.co.uk/sciencetech/article-2584738/Now-THATS
-open-plan-office-New-pictures-reveal-Facebooks-hacker-campus
-house-10-000-workers-ONE-room.html.

"facilitate communication and idea flow": Konnikova, Maria. "The
Open-Office Trap." *The New Yorker*, January 7, 2014. http://www
.newyorker.com/business/currency/the-open-office-trap.

"Open plan is pretty spectacular": Stevenson, Seth. "The Boss with No
Office." *Slate*, May 4, 2014. http://www.slate.com/articles/busi
ness/psychology_of_management/2014/05/open_plan_offices
_the_new_trend_in_workplace_design.1.html.

"We encourage people to stay out in the open": Savitz, Eric. "Jack
Dorsey: Leadership Secrets of Twitter and Square." Forbes, October 17, 2012. http://www.forbes.com/sites/ericsavitz/2012/10/17/
jack-dorsey-the-leadership-secrets-of-twitter-and-square/3/.

The *New Yorker* quotes about Building 20, as well as general background
and lists of inventions, come from the following 2012 *New Yorker*
article, combined to a lesser degree with the author's firsthand experience with such lore while at MIT: Lehrer, Jonah. "Groupthink."
The New Yorker, January 30, 2012. http://www.newyorker.com/
magazine/2012/01/30/groupthink.

"Traveling the hall's length" and the information on Mervin Kelly
and his goals for Bell Labs's Murray Hill campus: Gertner, Jon.
"True Innovation." *New York Times*, February 25, 2012. http://
www.nytimes.com/2012/02/26/opinion/sunday/innovation-and
-the-bell-labs-miracle.html.

A nice summary history of the invention of the transistor can be found in
"Transistorized!" at PBS's website: http://www.pbs.org/transistor/
album1/. A more detailed history can be found in Chapter 7 of
Walter Isaacson's 2014 book, *The Innovators*. New York: Simon
and Schuster.

Execute Like a Business

"How do I do this?": from pages xix–xx of McChesney, Chris, Sean
Covey, and Jim Huling. *The 4 Disciplines of Execution*. New York:
Simon and Schuster, 2004.

Clayton Christensen also talks more about his experience with Andy
Grove in a July–August 2010 *Harvard Business Review* article,
"How Will You Measure Your Life?" that he later expanded into

a book of the same name: http://hbr.org/2010/07/how-will-you
-measure-your-life/ar/1.

"The more you try to do": from page 10 of McChesney, Covey, and
Huling, *The 4 Disciplines of Execution*.

"If you want to win the war for attention": Brooks, David. "The
Art of Focus." *New York Times*, June 3, 2013. http://www
.nytimes.com/2014/06/03/opinion/brooks-the-art-of-focus.html
?hp&rref=opinion&_r=2.

"When you receive them": from page 12 of McChesney, Covey, and
Huling, *The 4 Disciplines of Execution*.

"People play differently when they're keeping score": Ibid., 12.

"a rhythm of regular and frequent meetings" and **"execution really
happens"**: Ibid., 13.

Be Lazy

"I am not busy" and **"Idleness is not just a vacation"**: Kreider, Tim.
"The Busy Trap." *New York Times*, June 30, 2013. http://opinionator
.blogs.nytimes.com/2012/06/30/the-busy-trap/.

Much (though not all) of the research cited to support the value of downtime was first brought to my attention through a detailed *Scientific American* article on the subject: Jabr, Ferris. "Why Your Brain
Needs More Downtime." *Scientific American*, October 15, 2013.
http://www.scientificamerican.com/article/mental-downtime/.

"The scientific literature has emphasized": from the abstract of
Dijksterhuis, Ap, Maarten W. Bos, Loran F. Nordgren, and Rick
B. van Baaren, "On Making the Right Choice: The Deliberation
-Without-Attention Effect." *Science* 311.5763 (2006): 1005–1007.

The attention restoration theory study described in the text: Berman,
Marc G., John Jonides, and Stephen Kaplan. "The Cognitive
Benefits of Interacting with Nature." *Psychological Science* 19.12
(2008): 1207–1212.

I called this study "frequently cited" based on the more than four hundred citations identified by Google Scholar as of November 2014.

An online article where Berman talks about this study and ART more
generally (the source of my Berman quotes): Berman, Marc. "Berman
on the Brain: How to Boost Your Focus." Huffington Post, February
2, 2012. http://www.huffingtonpost.ca/marc-berman/attention
-restoration-theory-nature_b_1242261.html.

Kaplan, Rachel, and Stephen Kaplan. *The Experience of Nature: A Psychological Perspective*. Cambridge: Cambridge University Press, 1989.

Ericsson, K.A., R.T. Krampe, and C. Tesch-Römer. "The Role of Deliberate Practice in the Acquisition of Expert Performance." *Psychological Review* 100.3 (1993): 363–406.

"Committing to a specific plan for a goal": from Masicampo, E.J., and Roy F. Baumeister. "Consider It Done! Plan Making Can Eliminate the Cognitive Effects of Unfulfilled Goals." *Journal of Personality and Social Psychology* 101.4 (2011): 667.

Rule #2

My estimate of "hundreds of thousands" of daily Talmud studiers comes from an article by Shmuel Rosner, "A Page a Day," *New York Times*, August 1, 2012 (http://latitude.blogs.nytimes.com/2012/08/01/considering-seven-and-a-half-years-of-daily-talmud-study/), as well as my personal correspondence with Adam Marlin.

"So we have scales that allow us to divide" and **"The people we talk with continually said"**: Clifford Nass's May 10, 2013, interview with Ira Flatow, on NPR's *Talk of the Nation: Science Friday* show. Audio and transcript are available online: "The Myth of Multitasking." http://www.npr.org/2013/05/10/182861382/the-myth-of-multitasking. In a tragic twist, Nass died unexpectedly just six months after this interview.

Don't Take Breaks from Distraction. Instead Take Breaks from Focus.

Powers, William. *Hamlet's BlackBerry: Building a Good Life in a Digital Age*. New York: Harper, 2010.

"Do what Thoreau did": "Author Disconnects from Communication Devices to Reconnect with Life." *PBS NewsHour*, August 16, 2010. http://www.pbs.org/newshour/bb/science-july-dec10-hamlets_08-16/.

Work Like Teddy Roosevelt

The general information about Theodore Roosevelt's Harvard habits comes from Edmund Morris's fantastic biography: Morris, Edmund. *The Rise of Theodore Roosevelt*. New York: Random House, 2001. In

particular, pages 61–65 include Morris's catalog of Roosevelt's col-
legiate activities and an excerpt from a letter from Roosevelt to his
mother that outlines his work habits. The specific calculation that
Roosevelt dedicates a quarter of his typical day to schoolwork comes
from page 64.

"amazing array of interests": from page 64 of Morris, *Rise of Theodore
Roosevelt*.

The positive receipt of Roosevelt's book by the *Nuttall Bulletin* comes
from Morris's endnotes: in particular, note 37 in the chapter titled
"The Man with the Morning in His Face."

"one of the most knowledgeable": from page 67 of Morris, *Rise of
Theodore Roosevelt*. I ascribed this assessment to Morris, though
this is somewhat indirect, as Morris here is actually arguing that
Roosevelt's father, after the publication of *The Summer Birds of the
Adirondacks*, must have felt this about his son.

"The amount of time he spent at his desk": from page 64 of Morris,
Rise of Theodore Roosevelt.

Memorize a Deck of Cards

Quotes from Daniel Kilov came from personal correspondence. Some
background on his story was taken from his online biography, http://
mentalathlete.wordpress.com/about/, and Lieu Thi Pham. "In Mel-
bourne, Memory Athletes Open Up Shop." ZDNet, August 21, 2013.
http://www.smartplanet.com/blog/global-observer/in-melbourne
-memory-athletes-open-up-shop/. More on Kilov's scores (memory
feats) from his two medal-winning championship bouts can be found
on the World Memory Statistics website: http://www.world-memory
-statistics.com/competitor.php?id=1102.

Foer, Joshua. *Moonwalking with Einstein: The Art and Science of Remembering Everything*. New York: Penguin, 2011.

"We found that one of the biggest differences": Carey, Benedict.
"Remembering, as an Extreme Sport." *New York Times* Well Blog,
May 19, 2014.

For more interesting connections between memorization and general
thought, see: *The Art of Memory*, by Frances A. Yates, which was
first published in 1966. The most accessible version seems to be the
handsome 2001 reprint by the University of Chicago Press.

Rule #3

"the most connected man in the world"; "I was burnt out"; "By the end of that first week"; "The end came too soon"; and general information about Baratunde Thurston's experiment: from the Baratunde Thurston article "#UnPlug" that appeared in the July–August 2013 issue of *Fast Company*. http://www.fastcompany.com/3012521/unplug/baratunde-thurston-leaves-the-internet.

The reference to Thurston's Twitter usage refers to the tweets on March 13, 2014, from the Twitter handle @Baratunde.

"Entertainment was my initial draw"; "[When] I first joined"; and **"[I use] Facebook because"**: drawn from comments sections of the following two blog posts I wrote in the fall of 2013:

- "Why I'm (Still) Not Going to Join Facebook: Four Arguments That Failed to Convince Me." http://calnewport.com/blog/2013/10/03/why-im-still-not-going-to-join-facebook-four-arguments-that-failed-to-convince-me/.
- "Why I Never Joined Facebook." http://calnewport.com/blog/2013/09/18/why-i-never-joined-facebook/.

For more on Forrest Pritchard and Smith Meadows Farms: http://smithmeadows.com/.

Apply the Law of the Vital Few to Your Internet Habits

"Who says my fans want to hear from me": from a Malcolm Gladwell talk that took place at the International Digital Publishing Forum as part of the 2013 BookExpo America Convention, held in May 2013, in New York City. A summary of the talk, including the quotes excerpted in this chapter, and some video excerpts, can be found in "Malcolm Gladwell Attacks NYPL: 'Luxury Condos Would Look Wonderful There,'" Huffington Post, May 29, 2013. http://www.huffingtonpost.com/2013/05/29/malcolm-gladwell-attacks-_n_3355041.html.

"I don't tweet" and **"It's amazing how overly accessible"**: from the following Michael Lewis interview: Allan, Nicole. "Michael Lewis: What I Read." The Wire, March 1, 2010. http://www.thewire.com/entertainment/2010/03/michael-lewis-what-i-read/20129/.

"And now, nearly a year later": from "Why Twitter Will Endure," by David Carr for the *New York Times* in January 2010: http://www .nytimes.com/2010/01/03/weekinreview/03carr.html.

"Twitter is crack for media addicts": from an online opinion piece written for the *New Yorker* website: Packer, George. "Stop the World." *The New Yorker*, January 29, 2010. http://www.newyorker.com/ online/blogs/georgepacker/2010/01/stop-the-world.html.

The law of the vital few is discussed in many sources. Richard Koch's 1998 book, *The 80/20 Principle* (New York: Crown, 1998), seems to have helped reintroduce the idea to a business market. Tim Ferriss's 2007 mega-seller, *The 4-Hour Workweek* (New York: Crown, 2007), popularized it further, especially among the technology entrepreneur community. The Wikipedia page on the Pareto principle has a good summary of various places where this general idea applies (I drew many of my examples from here): http:// en.wikipedia.org/wiki/Pareto_principle.

Quit Social Media

"Everything's more exciting when it's a party" and general information on Ryan Nicodemus's "packing party": "Day 3: Packing Party." The Minimalists. http://www.theminimalists.com/21days/day3/.

Average number of Twitter followers statistic comes from: "Average Twitter User Is an American Woman with an iPhone and 208 Followers." *Telegraph*, October 11, 2012. http://www.telegraph.co.uk/technology/ news/9601327/Average-Twitter-user-is-an-an-American-woman -with-an-iPhone-and-208-followers.html.

Take this statistic with a grain of salt. A small number of Twitter users have such a large following that the average skews high. Presumably the median would be much lower. But then again, both statistics include users who signed up just to try out the service or read tweets, and who made no serious attempt to ever gain followers or write tweets. If we confined our attention to those who actually tweet and want followers, then the follower numbers would be higher.

Don't Use the Internet to Entertain Yourself

"Take the case of a Londoner who works"; **"great and profound mistake"**; **"during those sixteen hours he is free"**; and **"What? You say that full energy"**: from Chapter 4 in Bennett, Arnold. *How to*

Live on 24 Hours a Day. Originally published in 1910. Quotes are from the free version of the text maintained in HTML format at Project Gutenberg: http://www.gutenberg.org/files/2274/2274-h/2274-h.htm.

Rule #4

"People should enjoy the weather in the summer" and general notes on Jason Fried's decision to move 37signals (now Basecamp) to a four-day workweek: "Workplace Experiments: A Month to Yourself." Signal v. Noise, May 31, 2012. https://signalvnoise.com/posts/3186-workplace-experiments-a-month-to-yourself.

"Packing 40 hours into four days": from a Forbes.com critique of Fried: Weiss, Tara. "Why a Four-Day Work Week Doesn't Work." Forbes. August 18, 2008. www.forbes.com/2008/08/18/careers-leadership-work-leadership-cx_tw_0818workweek.html.

"The point of the 4-day work week is" and **"Very few people work even 8 hours a day"**: from Fried's response on his company's blog: "Forbes Misses the Point of the 4-Day Work Week." Signal v. Noise, August 20, 2008. http://signalvnoise.com/posts/1209-forbes-misses-the-point-of-the-4-day-work-week.

"I'd take 5 days in a row": from Fried's company's blog: "Workplace Experiments." https://signalvnoise.com/posts/3186-workplace-experiments-a-month-to-yourself.

"How can we afford to": from an Inc.com article: Fried, Jason. "Why I Gave My Company a Month Off." Inc., August 22, 2012. http://www.inc.com/magazine/201209/jason-fried/why-company-a-month-off.html.

The notes on how many hours a day of deliberate practice are possible come from page 370 of: Ericsson, K.A., R.T. Krampe, and C. Tesch-Römer. "The Role of Deliberate Practice in the Acquisition of Expert Performance." *Psychological Review* 100.3 (1993): 363–406.

Schedule Every Minute of Your Day

The statistics about British TV habits come from this *Guardian* article, by Mona Chalabi, published on October 8, 2013: "Do We Spend More Time Online or Watching TV?" http://www.theguardian.com/politics/reality-check/2013/oct/08/spend-more-time-online-or-watching-tv-internet.

The Laura Vanderkam article in the *Wall Street Journal*: "Overestimating Our Overworking," May 29, 2009, http://online.wsj.com/news/articles/SB124355233998464405.

"I think you far understate": from comment #6 of the blog post "Deep Habits: Plan Your Week in Advance," August 8, 2014. http://calnewport.com/blog/2014/08/08/deep-habits-plan-your-week-in-advance.

Finish Your Work by Five Thirty

"Scary myths and scary data abound" and general information about Radhika Nagpal's fixed-schedule productivity habit: "The Awesomest 7-Year Postdoc or: How I Learned to Stop Worrying and Love the Tenure-Track Faculty Life," *Scientific American*, July 21, 2013. http://blogs.scientificamerican.com/guest-blog/2013/07/21/the-awesomest-7-year-postdoc-or-how-i-learned-to-stop-worrying-and-love-the-tenure-track-faculty-life/.

Matt Welsh's quote about typical travel for junior faculty: "The Fame Trap." Volatile and Decentralized, August 4, 2014. http://matt-welsh.blogspot.com/2014/08/the-fame-trap.html.

The issue of *Science* where Radhika Nagpal's work appears on the cover: http://www.sciencemag.org/content/343/6172.toc; *Science* 343.6172 (February 14, 2014): 701–808.

Become Hard to Reach

"we are slowly eroding our ability to explain": from page 13 of Freeman, John. *The Tyranny of E-mail: The Four-Thousand-Year Journey to Your Inbox*. New York: Scribner, 2009.

To see my sender filters in action: http://calnewport.com/contact/.

"So, when I emailed Cal to ask if he": Glei, Jocelyn. "Stop the Insanity: How to Crush Communication Overload." 99U, http://99u.com/articles/7002/stop-the-insanity-how-to-crush-communication-overload.

"At some point, the number of people reaching out" and more details on Clay Herbert and Antonio Centeno's filters: Simmons, Michael. "Open Relationship Building: The 15-Minute Habit That Transforms Your Network." Forbes, June 24, 2014. http://www.forbes.com/sites/michaelsimmons/2014/06/24/open-relationship-building-the-15-minute-habit-that-transforms-your-network/.

Notice, this Forbes.com article also talks about my own sender filter
habit. (I suggested the name "sender filter" to the article's author,
Michael Simmons, who is also a longtime friend of mine.)

See Antonio's filters in action: http://www.realmenrealstyle.com/contact/.

"Develop the habit of letting small bad things happen": from
Tim Ferriss' blog: "The Art of Letting Bad Things Happen."
The Tim Ferriss Experiment, October 25, 2007. http://fourhour
workweek.com/2007/10/25/weapons-of-mass-distractions
-and-the-art-of-letting-bad-things-happen/.

Conclusion

"a prodigious feat of concentration": from an article for the *Harvard Gazette*: Isaacson, Walter. "Dawn of a Revolution," September 2013. http://news.harvard.edu/gazette/story/2013/09/dawn
-of-a-revolution/.

"The one trait that differentiated [Gates from Allen] was focus":
Isaacson, Walter. *The Innovators*. New York: Simon and Schuster,
2014. The quote came from 9:55 into Chapter 6 of Part 2 in the
unabridged Audible.com audio version of the book.

The details of the Bill Gates story came mainly from Isaacson, "Dawn
of a Revolution," article, which Walter Isaacson excerpted (with
modification) from his *Innovators*. I also pulled some background
details, however, from Stephen Manes's excellent 1994 business
biography. Manes, Stephen. *Gates: How Microsoft's Mogul Rein-
vented an Industry—and Made Himself the Richest Man in America*.
New York: Doubleday, 1992.

Newport, Cal. *So Good They Can't Ignore You: Why Skill Trumps Passion
in the Quest for Work You Love*. New York: Business Plus, 2012.

You can find a list of my computer science publications, organized
by year, at my academic website: http://people.cs.georgetown
.edu/~cnewport. The publications from my year of living deeply
are listed under 2014. Notice that theoretical computer scientists,
like myself, publish mainly in competitive conferences, not journals, and that we tend to list authors alphabetically, not in order of
contribution.

"I'll live the focused life": from page 14 of Gallagher, *Rapt*.

Index